CRE▲TIVE
HOMEOWNER®

Best
Signature
Baths

CREATIVE HOMEOWNER®, Mahwah, New Jersey

First published in book form in 2012 by

CRE▲TIVE
HOMEOWNER®

A Division of Federal Marketing Corp.
Mahwah, NJ

Signature Kitchens & Baths Magazine is published by Magnolia Media Group

VICE PRESIDENT & PUBLISHER: Timothy O. Bakke
EDITOR: Kathie Robitz
ART DIRECTOR: David Geer
PRODUCTION COORDINATOR: Sara M. Markowitz
DIGITAL IMAGING SPECIALIST: Mary Dolan

Current Printing (last digit)
10 9 8 7 6 5 4 3

Manufactured in the United States of America

Best Signature Baths
Library of Congress Control Number: 2011925584
ISBN-10: 1-58011-532-2
ISBN-13: 978-1-58011-532-2

CREATIVE HOMEOWNER®
A Division of Federal Marketing Corp.
One International Blvd., Suite 400
Mahwah, NJ 07458
www.creativehomeowner.com

Planet Friendly Publishing
- ✓ Made in the United States
- ✓ Printed on Recycled Paper
  Text: 10%   Cover: 10%
  Learn more: www.greenedition.org

GREEN EDITION®

At Creative Homeowner we're committed to producing books in an earth-friendly manner and to helping our customers make greener choices.

Manufacturing books in the United States ensures compliance with strict environmental laws and eliminates the need for international freight shipping, a major contributor to global air pollution.

And printing on recycled paper helps minimize our consumption of trees, water, and fossil fuels. Best Signature Kitchens was printed on paper made with 10% post-consumer waste. According to the Environmental Paper Network's Paper Calculator, by using this innovative paper instead of conventional papers we achieved the following environmental benefits:

Trees Saved: 19

Water Saved: 8,988 gallons

Solid Waste Eliminated: 602 pounds

Greenhouse Gas Emissions Eliminated: 1,657 pounds

For more information on our environmental practices, please visit us online at www.creativehomeowner.com/green

CONTENTS

beautiful basins

While lavs have always been a bathroom staple, this selection showcases stunning examples that are anything but commonplace. // *Compiled by Haley Owens and Alison Rich*

↑ Drop-Dead Gorgeous //
Stone Forest has upped the creative ante with this introduction to its popular SYNC collection. Pictured here in stunning multicolored onyx, it is also available in water-resistant bamboo and honed basalt. Stone Forest, www.stoneforest.com.

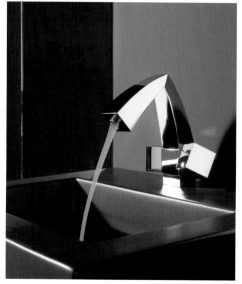

← Modern Masterpiece //
Though the low-flow Fontaine faucet from GRAFF may look more like an Art Deco piece than a bathroom staple, it packs a powerful punch behind its enchanting façade. Inside the faucet's bold outer design of strong lines are modern high-tech features, such as the water-saving aerator. The aerator, which reduces water flow to 1.5 gpm, is just part of what makes this modern masterpiece an irresistible addition to any discerning homeowner's collection. GRAFF, www.graff-faucets.com.

↑ **Spotlight the Sink //** Considering the frequency of use, when it comes to your bathroom sink, it's a shame not to have a beautiful basin. And a handsome new lav can instantly dress up any bathroom. One style sure to impress, LAUFEN's new ILBAGNOALESSI One TUNA washbasin is an imaginative, timeless piece that has just the right touch of beauty and uniqueness. Borrowing from the graceful curves of its namesake, its fluid, elongated lines offer an updated shape that marries well with the traditional clean white finish. This modern-meets-classic cohesiveness makes this ceramic sink certainly suitable to spotlight. LAUFEN, www.laufen.com/usa.

→ **Beauty and Brains //** ShowHouse by Moen has combined form and function in its new Fina bathroom collection. Offering homeowners both beauty and brains, the compilation not only features soft, modern-style cues with high-arc spouts and lever handles but also offers the first WaterSense-labeled lavatory faucets from the ShowHouse brand, indicating the spigots have met the Environmental Protection Agency's new guidelines for water-efficient products. ShowHouse by Moen, www.showhouse.moen.com.

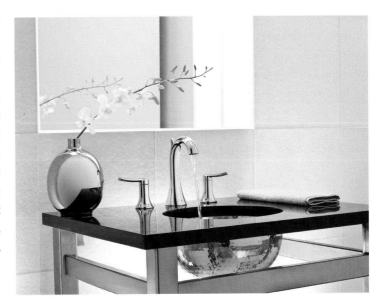

Bronze Mettle // This graceful crescent-shape lav, the Lunette Bronze Vessel, eclipses other sink designs of its kind. Created by Santa Fe artist David Hoptman, the artfully styled basin boasts a textured surface that gives rise to its sculptural silhouette and ethereal aesthetic. How's that for beauty that beams? Stone Forest, www.stoneforest.com.

Elegance Meets Edge // The new trough-style Petra Double Sink by MTI Whirlpools blends a stylishly spare motif with the resilience of solid-surface construction. Nonporous and naturally stain resistant, the material wipes sparkling clean in seconds. Available in one-piece construction, white or biscuit, and matte or gloss finish, the Petra can be installed atop a vanity or partially recessed into the countertop. MTI Whirlpools, www.mtiwhirlpools.com.

Liquid Assets // For a top-rate tap that flows with flexibility, the Cono basin and vanity combination is the hands-down winner. The basin is ceramic with a texturous finish. It comes in numerous colors. Shown here atop a wall-hung double vanity in teak, it is part of the CLO Collection. Hastings Tile & Bath, www.hastingstilebath.com.

→ **Breathtaking Bamboo //**
Inspired by a salad bowl already produced by Totally Bamboo, this unique bamboo sink is breaking the mold. The Bamboo Vessel Lavatory Sink is the first—but not the last—of its kind. Craftsmen hand-turn each sink on a large lathe, creating a variety of shapes and sizes. Totally Bamboo, www.totallybamboo.com.

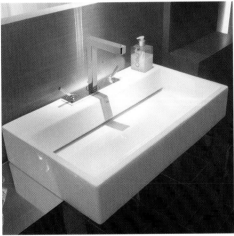

↑ **Hidden Treasure //** Flaunting maximum style cloaked in a mimimalist profile, Deca's new Concealed Waste Slab Basin showcases its sleek-lined silhouette while ingeniously hiding the drain from view. The avant-garde lav conceals the drain behind a small vent located at the back of the basin. Deca, www.deca-us.com.

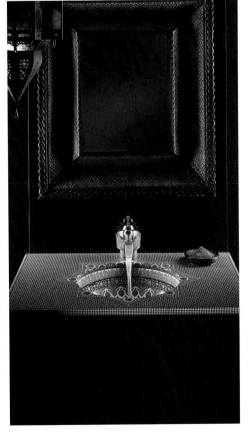

← **Moroccan Mosaic //** Create a fabulously unique bath or powder room with Kohler's Marrakesh lav, which is featured in the Camber countertop. The design was inspired by Moorish mosaics discovered in a Moroccan courtyard and by artwork in the country's Blue Mosque. Kohler, www.kohler.com.

Branching Out // While Linkasink's initial product offerings were limited to copper sinks, the company has expanded over the past 13 years to include designs that stretch the imagination. Offering a variety of high-end finishes—such as copper, cloisonné, carved marble, cast metal, porcelain, and bronze—Linkasink broke the mold with this distinctive "tree trunk" bowl. A whimsical yet realistic interpretation, it's made of carved marble; the interior is finished with mosaic tile. Linkasink, www.linkasink.com.

Blissful Basin // Stone Forest's brilliance with onyx shines through yet again with the elegant Infinity Pedestal sink. This alluring cylindrical design makes a striking statement. Stone Forest, www.stoneforest.com.

Washed Up // The Pure Stone line from Villeroy & Boch is an innovative way to give your bath a sense of the outdoors and was inspired by water-washed rocks and pebbles. The range of surfaces and finishes evoke a feeling of natural stone. Villeroy & Boch, www.villeroy-boch.com.

Star-Worthy Sink // Recycled glass scraps look heavenly in Alchemy's new Celestial Series sinks. Created in a warm autumnal palette of fragmented glass shards and pebbles, the Cosmic Burst, Terra Nova, and Mosaic models feature a brilliant palette. All of the beautiful basins are original artisan-crafted designs. Alchemy Glass & Light, www.alchemyglass.com.

← Drowning the Competition //
Leading the marketplace in both style and ingenuity, it's no surprise that Watermark Design's Titanium faucet was recently installed in the City College of New York's "Solar Roof Pod," the school's first entry into the U.S. Department of Energy's 2011 Solar Decathlon Competition. Though the faucet boasts a sleek modern design, it's more than just a looker—it contains water-saving elements with a hydro-progressive water control feature that is sure to make any eco-savvy consumer swoon. Watermark Designs, www.watermark-designs.com.

→ Color-Saturated Stream // If you're looking for an avant-garde element for the bathroom, your search ends with the HANSACANYON. The water stream is illuminated and varies in color from cool blue to warm red to reflect the water's temperature change. And the design casts an entirely new light on your water experience, as it is controlled electronically via a touch pad; no control technology is visible. So all you are left with is the minimalist cool chrome of the faucets and illuminated water in a fluid free fall. HANSACANYON, www.hansa.com.

← Streams of Consciousness // The simplicity of the hand-carved, hand-smoothed Italian marble Siena Tamburo Vessel Sink is awash in quiet elegance. Understated earth tones and distinct striations convey an effortless feel that beckons bliss to the bath. A carved cavity in the back allows for easy installation while cleverly cloaking the plumbing underneath. Stone Forest, www.stoneforest.com.

flower power

TURN OVER A NEW DESIGN LEAF WITH THESE FLORAL-PATTERNED TILES THAT HAVE A LASTING LOOK AND WON'T WILT WHEN THE SEASONS SWITCH. **BY ALISON RICH**

Though welcome in landscapes, floral motifs are sometimes met with some resistance indoors. What spurs this hesitation? Perhaps some homeowners cringe as they conjure images of dowdy patterns of the past, and maybe others worry their floral infatuation will fade by fall. But fear not. Available in tile form, these beauties don't feature the garish go-to patterns of old, with their brash bouquets and overwrought, saccharine-sweet motifs. Instead, today's new crop of flowered tiles is tasteful and understated—if not a little whimsical and unique.

But whether they're infused with colors—think the eternal paintings of Georgia O'Keefe—or display a more restrained palette, these Art Deco-inspired designs are sure to make any bathroom look cheerful year-round. Here, we offer up a design museum of sorts, presenting three differing takes on this look. After admiring these fresh picks, we're sure you'll agree: there's not a single wallflower in this beautiful bunch.

TULI ART If your drab bathroom is a thorn in your side—or even if it just needs some minor updating—this cheerful tile by Hastings Tile &

Bath, designed by Ronald Van Der Hirst for Bardelli, might be just the thing. With glossy pops of orange, red, and purple, the hand-painted tilework is a lighthearted creation guaranteed to liven up your lavatory in a most delightful way.

By turns contemporary and traditional, the outsized tulips invite the eye upward, adding a sense of height to even the smallest of spots. The titles are on a single wall, ensuring a makeover look that's definitely not overdone.

TULI-TULI Also nothing to sneeze at, Hastings' Tuli-Tuli is yet another option for putting your signature on your new bath's design. The hand-painted tiles speak volumes, but do so in hushed tones.

Light and airy, the flowers seemingly rise from the floor, grounding the minimalistic design in a garden of timeless style. Much the same as in an outdoor flowerbed, the smaller tulips alongside the tub (not shown) serve as a floral border, highlighting this section of the room while adding visual interest to the entire bathscape. In the bathroom pictured opposite, the black-and-white composition plays off the muted fixtures, straight lines, and fair-hued wood floors. But these Tuli-Tuli tiles would look just as lovely in a differently composed space—testament to the product's design flexibility.

VHC SERIES Floral motifs in today's ultra-modern bathrooms? Numerous fixtures echo the contemporary vernacular, but finding complementary tiles from the available inventory hasn't been as effortless an undertaking—until now, that is. Check out Hastings Tile & Bath's VHC Series, also designed by Ronald Van Der Hirst and shown on page 12 in a blocky mix of red-and-black tiles festooned with roses.

But these aren't your grandma's old-fashioned flowers. Resembling glamorous artwork worthy of top billing at any premier gallery, this new tile is at once fashionable and long lasting. Befitting of spare spaces that demand a crowning swath of color, the VHC boasts a wither-proof look crafted—as are the other tiles here—to stand the test of time.

So when you're rooting around for a flower-inspired bathroom tile that will look as lovely tomorrow as it does today, consider these options with beauty that stems from an atypical arrangement of design stability, ingenuity, and practicality. «

soak up the sun

MOVING THE SPA INTO THE OPEN AIR, THESE EIGHT OUTDOOR SHOWER AND BATH DESIGNS
ARE SURE TO LEAVE YOU SUN-DRENCHED AND SQUEAKY CLEAN. **BY NICOLE M. PEARCE**

ONCE CONSIDERED a luxury reserved for a privileged few, an outdoor bath or shower has now become a quintessential addition to the landscape. Many homeowners have realized that the addition not only serves a useful function but provides a sense of completion to the backyard as well. Like all design considerations, however, this one, too, must balance the existing environment. Just as a contemporary faucet complements a sleek and modern bathroom, so should an outdoor bath or shower enhance—not detract from—the surroundings. Delve into this diverse collection of design choices to see which one best matches your outdoor space.

THE MINIMALIST: FS3 BY VOLA The FS3 by Vola, **left,** is the ultimate outdoor shower for those who appreciate simple yet elegant construction. Its geometric appearance serves as an interesting accent in the landscape, resembling a freestanding sculpture more than a backyard shower. The design is incredibly slender, yet it's made to be powerful, providing an intense curtain of water equipped with precise temperature regulation. A handshower feature gives bathers

side-mounted controls offer complete regulation of the overhead spray and a soothing foot shower. Its mirrorlike finish reflects the beauty of the outdoors, allowing the device to also act as an artistic accessory. But this outdoor shower isn't just handsome. Its solid construction ensures it will remain not only beautiful but also perfectly functional season after season. JACLO, www.jaclo.com.

THE CONTORTIONIST: SUNDECK BY DURAVIT

Imagine stepping onto the patio and soaking in the sun while soaking in the tub. With Sundeck by Duravit (not shown) , this paradise is within reach. The luxurious tub is much more than meets the eye. When it is not in use, a cushioned cover seals the top to create a comfortable sunning deck. And what's more, when the seal is closed, the water remains warm while the tub is filling. An overflow channel prevents accidental overfilling. Optional whirlpool jets, LED lighting, and a remote control take bathing to the next level. The weather-resistant laminate enclosure ensures that the vessel will remain sturdy and beautiful for years to come. Duravit, www.duravit.com.

THE ARTIST: WAVE BY DESIGNERZEIT

Do more than just shower outdoors—make a statement with Wave by Designerzeit (not shown). The structure's graceful curves are designed to evoke the reposeful environment of the ocean, and its multiple sprayheads with soothing water pressure offer complete relaxation. Essential to this device is its external control panel, which provides easy-to-use yet precise control over the sprayheads and their temperatures. A foot fountain pours a heavy stream of water to clean and soothe tired feet. Buyers may choose between two sprayheads: a swiveling option for precise directional control or three levels of massage. Designerzeit, www.designerzeit.com.

THE TRADITIONALIST: MEDINA BY D'UN JARDIN À L'AUTRE

The charm of the Medina by D'un Jardin à l'Autre (not shown) will add a classic touch to any outdoor environment. This outdoor shower features a decorative enclosure made of fire forged-iron scrollwork adjustable panels. A hot-water regulator ensures that the water temperature remains comfortable throughout the bathing experience. The accessories are available in brass for a seamless appearance or stainless steel for visual interest. And while the panels may appear to be delicate, the entire structure is treated with an antirust agent to form a protective film to preserve it summer after summer. D'un Jardin à l'Autre, www.douches-de-jardins.com.

even more control over their experience. The design comes in three durable and attractive materials: stainless steel, chrome, and brushed chrome. Vola, www.vola.com.

THE CONSERVATIONIST: ENERGY AND DADA BY ARKEMA

Whether you keep green living as your household's top priority or would just like to make a low-carbon-emission addition, the Energy series by Arkema (not shown) is a future-friendly choice. This smart, sustainable shower uses a photovoltaic panel to transform the sun into a hardy stream of hot or cold water for the bather. A special foot shower provides a simple spray to clean away dirt, grass, and sand. The thin, sleek design with chromatic nozzle and controls will blend in well with any landscape, and a choice of three colors—slate, teal, and white—are sure to match your milieu. The DADA series offers all of the eco-friendly features, but with bold touches of color: bright purple, pink, and orange. Arkema, www.arkemadesign.com.

THE MODERNIST: ARC COLUMN ALLEGRO BY JACLO

Seemingly structured out of a solid piece of stainless steel, the Arc Column Allegro by JACLO, **above,** adds modern elegance to the backyard. The tall arced form is topped with a tilting rain-tile showerhead, easily adjustable for a perfect angle. Sleek

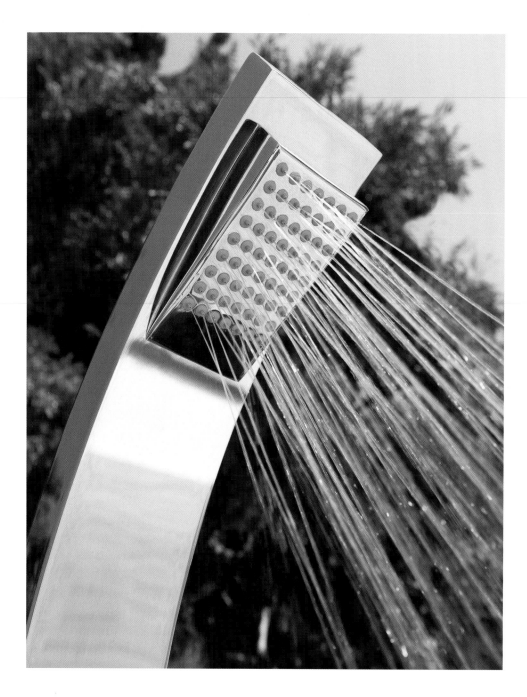

THE NATURALIST: WAIMEA BY DESIGNERIZE IT For backyards that are staying true to organic design elements such as waterfalls, natural stone, and plenty of lush greenery, this is a must-have. Designed to replicate the look of a tall stalk of bamboo, this shower is actually constructed from teak (not shown), a natural weather-resistant material. A large showerhead, **above**, extends gracefully from the uppermost portion of the shower, soaking the bather in a deluge of water. Retro-inspired cross-handle stainless-steel hardware adds a classic touch. The shower's circular base allows for installation on grass, reducing the worry of a soggy lawn or muddy toes. Honeymoon, www.designerizeit.com.

THE REALIST: OUTDOOR SHOWER BY ORVIS This handsome, practical shower (not shown) is constructed with nyatoh wood—a naturally water- and weather-resistant material. It can be treated with teak oil or allowed to age naturally. The shower is easy to assemble, and the showerhead is adjustable to accommodate the height of the bather. A large bottom panel provides slip-proof footing. Upon assembly, simply connect the shower to a hose spigot to enjoy a crisp, cool, rain-like experience. Orvis, www.orvis.com. «

LAVISH LAVS

*Luxe materials and decadent designs elevate the bathroom
to a personal sanctuary of indulgent relaxation.*

// By Shalene Roberts

THG's Art Deco bathtub, www.thgusa.com

THG's Vogue faucet, www.thgusa.com

It was seen many years ago as a room of mere utilitarian necessity, but today's bathroom has evolved into an ultra-luxe retreat, an inner sanctum of serenity boasting tantalizing textures, sophisticated color palettes, and lavish accessories. And to top off this feast for the senses, discreetly integrated technology makes the bathroom one of the tech-savviest spaces in the home. Personal pampering has never been so good.

Gold Rush // Nothing evokes a sense of indulgence like gold. As one of the first metals ever to be mined, gold has always been equated with luxury. Since ancient times, this noble metal has bedecked palaces, tombs, relics, and the privileged members of society. Even into the early twentieth century, gold was the standard by which we measured the value of our currency. Gold doesn't whisper of wealth; gold is a bold display of prosperity. And nowhere else does it more blatantly speak of lavish indulgence than in the bathroom.

Designed by Parisian-based THG (www.thgusa.com), the bathtub on the previous page, part of the Marquise Collection, is the crown jewel for anyone seeking the sweet life. Created by artisans at THG, the tub was inspired by the the iconic china pattern of Bernardaud. (Established in Limoges, France, in 1863, Bernardaud continues to be a revered family-run company creating sought-after porcelain wares.) The tub would be at home in a French chateau. Featuring an intricate and beautifully hand-applied pattern, it is the ultimate expression of extravagance. And because the pattern is integrated into the bathing beauty itself, the tub is guaranteed not to peel or fade. In essence, it will age with splendor.

For homeowners who may be seeking less glitz than a gilded tub, THG and a variety of other bath manufacturers are offering gold tones in everything from faucets to countertop accessories. When combined with crystal or precious stones, gilded hardware imbues a bathroom with a magical, jewel-like quality. The THG Vogue collection combines gold with turquoise, chalcedon, gray agate, rose quartz, thulite, cornaline, smoky quartz, rock crystal, amethyst, or aragonite. The company's Marquise Collection also features a full suite of bathroom products, including two faucet models and coordinating accessories.

And though gold lends itself exceptionally well to chic, contemporary environments, it is also at home in Old World environments, especially when featuring a burnished, time-worn patina. Pairing well with black, white, or an array of hues, including both warm and cool color palettes, gold is the quintessential über-luxe material that will elevate any bathroom to a sanctuary of self indulgence.

THG's Passion Collection, www.thgusa.com

Hollywood Regency // Fueled by such famed designers as Kelly Wearstler, the 1930s Hollywood Regency style—a favorite of '30s-era screen stars and other fashionable luminaries of the day—is enjoying a dazzling resurgence. Defined by rich, bright colors in a glossy, lacquered sheen, loads of layered luxurious fabrics, polished metallics, and reflective glass surfaces, Hollywood Regency will instantly catapult any bathroom to the status of elegant, ultra-glam escape. Bathrooms that channel Hollywood's Golden Age will feature mirrored vanities with high-sheen, lacquered accents, extravagant chandeliers, and faucets and hardware featuring high-gloss silvery metallics.

THG's Passion Collection, **opposite and above**, featuring Bernardaud Porcelain, bespeaks of Tinsel Town glamour. Romantic and graceful, Passion has every can't-live-without Hollywood Regency-style feature and combines delicate vintage details with exquisite modern design. Pieces within the Passion Collection exude gracious living; the faucet combines the femininity of clover-shaped handles balanced by a right-angled, geometric spout. Accessories adorning the suite feature the Bernardaud mascot, the butterfly, in an intoxicating shade of jade. Any bathroom embellished with the ultra-elegant elements of this style will become a lustrous oasis.

THG's Passion Collection,
www.thgusa.com

Time-Worn Classics // Typified by textured
walls, tumbled stone, rustic ironwork, distressed
wood tones, and feminine scrolling curves,
Old World style remains popular. The raw earthi-
ness of Old World invites one to take pause; the
abundant use of natural materials creates a recon-
nection with the past and invokes a sense of cozy
warmth. And nowhere is this atmosphere more
welcome than in the bathroom.

A throwback to European design, the clean,
simple lines of the Atocha Soaking Bath by Diamond Spas, **left**, are graceful yet masculine. Constructed of 4-inch strips of welded copper, this tub
demands prominence, yet rouses an undeniable
sense of calm serenity. One dip into this tub, and
the sensory experience expands beyond sight. The
ends of the tub are crafted to cradle the shoulders
and back, and the tub measures a roomy 36 x 68
x 24 inches. The tub is the pièce de résistance in
any Euro-themed spalike retreat. Diamond Spas,
which specializes in the custom fabrication of
stainless-steel and copper aquatic products, custom-
designs them to fit the specific needs of each client. Its product lines are also composed mainly of
recycled sheet metal, making it as earth-friendly as
it is elegant. (www.diamondspas.com)

For the ultimate Old World organic sink
basin, Stone Forest offers the Veneto Pedestal
Sink in Multi-Color Onyx, **opposite**. The
sink was inspired by classic Italian design. Its
barrel-shaped basin is carved from single blocks
of multicolored onyx, and the sculptural piece
boasts a cavity in back that can accommodate a
light source to enhance the sink/pedestal's form.
(www.stoneforest.com)

Stone Forest's Veneto Pedestal Sink in Multi-Color Onyx, www.stoneforest.com

THG's Yoko Suite, www.thgusa.com

East Meets West // The influence of Eastern design can be seen in today's Zen-themed Western spas. The clean lines and soft, monochromatic color scheme of this design style invite you to shirk your burdens and slip into a state of relaxation. To pump up the energy in a Zen-inspired oasis, bold pops of contrasting color create an invigorating ambiance. The result is bold but subtle, striking yet serene. It is a space that awakens the senses in the morning and realigns them in the evenings.

Exemplifying the harmony and balance of this aesthetic is the Yoko Suite by THG. Inspired by the Japanese bath, this suite features lush, textural elements that contrast and complement. Intricate details epitomize the Cristal de Lalique Bambou, including a carved bamboo pattern and satin-finished carved Lalique crystal handles. The slender tub filler anchors the faucet, its geometric lines softened by curved edges. A stand-alone statement of style in its own right, the Yoko bathtub is lined in leather, which provides a textural complement to the metallic interior of the Vasque sink. Two rainfall

THG's Yoko Suite, www.thgusa.com

THG's Yoko Suite, www.thgusa.com

showerheads in the open-concept shower create a soothing experience where the cares of the
day melt away. An East-meets-West at-home
spa will elevate any bathroom to the caliber of
personal haven where tranquility and peaceful
repose are within easy reach.

No matter your stylistic preference—the lavish glitz of gold, the ultra-glamorous detailing of
Hollywood Regency, the well-worn timelessness
of Old World design, or the Zenlike environment of an Eastern-inspired personal retreat—
products with rich textural detailing, beautifully
hued patinas, and organic, natural design elements combine to take personal pampering to
new heights and make the bathroom the most
lavishly crafted space in the home. «

plumb perfect!

THESE SIX WATER-EFFICIENT SPOUTS ARE SUSTAINABLE WITH SINGLE-HANDLED STYLE.

JUST BECAUSE YOU want to save water—and the planet while you're at it—doesn't mean you have to scrimp on style. Store shelves are filled with fab faucets that offer a double benefit: not only do they look lovely, but these must-have fittings don't waste water. Here is our short list of six of the top single-handled bathroom taps destined to become permanent fixtures in today's earth-savvy shelters.

FLUID FASHION Swap your water-waster for this style-setter, which is dressing today's most en vogue—and in-the-know—lavatories. Part of a wave of single-handled lavatory faucets recently introduced into Moen's most popular collections, it was a welcomed addition to the Brantford line. Certified to conform with WaterSense criteria, Moen's alluring and environmentally responsible faucet sits pretty while preserving precious resources. Moen, www.moen.com.

IN HAUTE WATER If a bath remodel with a sustainable bent is on your radar, then the Metris C line of lavatory, bidet, and tub faucets will definitely make waves. A traditional-meets-mod motif merges with state-of-the-art engineering in this new series featuring Hansgrohe EcoRight technology to limit flow rates to 1.5 gallons per minute—a 30 percent saving over conventional lav faucets. The entire line is available in five finishes: rubbed bronze, brushed nickel, polished nickel, oil-rubbed bronze, and chrome. Hansgrohe, www.hansgrohe-usa.com.

THE GOLD STANDARD Adding a water-conserving faucet to your elegant eco-bath is but a dream no more, thanks to the Vibrant Moderne Polished Gold on Purist Single-Control faucet from Kohler. Shrouded in a minimalist, monoblock aesthetic, it's a shrewd spout that touts streamlined H_2O control and WaterSense certification, along with an air of gilt glam that's eternally in style. Definitely a water winner that's worth it. Kohler, www.kohler.com.

NO FUSS, NO MUSS Add a splash of style to your sink by adorning it with the Grohe Essence faucet, the epitome of sustainable chic. Cool, crisp lines amid a shimmery chrome finish accentuate its cylindrical shape and straightforward design. Stamped with the WaterSense seal of approval so you know it's good for the globe, the Essence puts out just the right amount of liquid (no squandered gallons here). Plus, built-in technical advancements make it smart and sexy. Grohe, www.groheamerica.com.

ECO LOGICAL For a pro-planet product with a transitional twist, Danze's Antioch collection fits the bill. Swanlike curves and a graceful handle design channel a distinctive feel that adapts well to any eco-conscious environmental. It's a faucet that overflows with style, without draining your budget … no wonder so many savings-conscious consumers are in a lather over it! Danze, www.danze.com.

SWING LOW Fluid's Swing suite of fixtures is just one of its eight new collections inspired by nature, art, or architecture. The rhythm of music is reflected in the flowing form of Swing faucets— their graceful curved lines are similar to the f-holes of a cello. The faucet is also incredibly efficient. When equipped with a low-flow aerator, it flows at 1.5 gallons per minute, a rate that has gained it WaterSense certification. Fluid, www.fluidfaucets.com.

warming trends

MELT AWAY YOUR STRESSES—AND HEAT UP YOUR STYLE!—WITH THESE BLISS-INDUCING, BATH-FRIENDLY FIREPLACES. **BY NICOLE M. HOLLAND**

This pass-through fireplace adds a warm glow to this bathroom by architect Lynn Taylor Lohr and designer Kari Demond of KLM Interiors.

THERE'S NOTHING MORE RELAXING THAN A TRIP TO THE SPA. To re-create that bliss at home, many homeowners have begun transforming their master bath into personal retreats—with one addition, in particular, that truly transforms a space into a resortlike escape: a fireplace. This amenity will provide not only soothing warmth but an abundance of visual interest as well.

THE HOT SPOT There are several considerations involved when making plans to add a fireplace to the bath. First is location. According to Jason Heffley, owner of Heffley's Hearth and Home, homeowners can get creative when it comes to positioning their fireplace. Some people place it above a soaking tub, while others install it between a pair of vanity mirrors. But perhaps the most common locale for a bathroom fireplace is situated between the master bedroom and bath. By using a see-through design, homeowners get the most out of the addition.

FEEL THE BURN The second consideration is choosing what kind of energy will fuel your flame: gas, wood, or electric. If you're planning on the popular see-through design, Heffley advises steering clear of a wood-burning unit, despite the outright appeal of crackling embers. The reason is simple: the bedroom and bath are usually very different in size, which results in an effect called "blowback" that can cause excess smoke to exit the chamber. Instead, he suggests using a gas system. This way, homeowners can easily control the size of the flame, which in turn controls the temperature.

ALL FIRED UP … OR NOT Third, consider your commitment to the process. If you want the outright luxury of a built-in fireplace, your designer or architect will be well-versed in the installation process—and you can truly customize the outcome. Architect James LaRue incorporated a sophisticated fireplace right above the bathtub for his client, **right**. The fire screen features elegant scrolls, and water fountains on either side of the hearth spill into the bath below.

If this kind of major addition isn't feasible, there are also several low-cost options that don't involve a major renovation. These four fireplaces are relatively easy to install and maintain—so you'll be basking in the glow before you know it:

» CLASSIC CONTENDER For those with more traditional tastes, the gas wall-mount Vittoria by the Victorian Fireplace Shop (www.gascoals.net) heats up a room with late 19th-century style. Homeowners can choose from a black or pewter finish customized with refined scroll insets. A thermostat allows you to maintain precise temperature control. The fireplace comes mounted on flat- or corner-style cabinets for extra storage.

» GET GLOWING Heat & Glo (www.heatnglo.com) offers a wide selection of gas, wood, and electric systems. The Metro 32 is slim with a small footprint—ideal for squeezing into a bath that's tight on space. The 32-inch viewing area provides a wide, high-definition view of the flame, while the sleek frame, available in a number of finishes, complements a modern milieu. Dress up the appearance with the addition of glass media, which glow when lit by the flame. And what could be better than manipulating the entire system right from your bathtub with a separate handheld control?

» THE GREAT DIVIDE For a truly attention-getting addition, look no further than the peninsula fireplace by Heatilator (www.heatilator.com). The dramatic flames can be viewed clearly from three sides, making it the perfect divider between the bedroom and the bath. The flame height is adjustable, which makes it simple to regulate just the right amount of heat and light. And with the IntelliFire ignition system, it's easy to keep bills within budget, as this optional feature saves energy during every fire.

The elements of water and fire combine to create a truly relaxing retreat in this bathroom by architect James LaRue.

» MIST OPPORTUNITY If having a real flame glowing in your oasis is a bit off-putting, there's an option that will suit your desire for fire, without the gas. The OptiMist by Dimplex (www.dimplex.com) is an electric fireplace that actually produces an illusion of the smoke and flicker of a wood-burning fireplace. This true-to-life depiction is created by a thin water mist that weaves throughout the furnace strategically lit from below. For a more dramatic effect, users can freely adjust the intensity of the mist. The unit comes equipped with a heater, which can be used to add soothing warmth to the space.

There's nothing quite like basking in the glow of a flickering flame after a long soak in the tub. No matter what option you choose—a gas fireplace near the tub or an electric one by the vanity—your new bath addition will be a toasty focal point for years to come. «

ALL DECKED OUT

Even the most detailed designs aren't fully finished without the final touch of decorative hardware.

// By Haley Owens

JUST AS ANY outfit is not a complete ensemble without a selection of style-boosting accessories, bathroom cabinetry can look downright undressed without its rightful ornamentation. The jewelry of home design, decorative hardware is a small detail that can lend a big impact, dressing up cabinetry from bare to beautiful. So as you look around your bathroom, ask yourself: is your hardware working it, or is your hardware hardly working? If you don't adore your adornments, it's time to pull out the old pulls and knock out the old knobs for a fresh set.

The good news is that with a screwdriver in hand, this style switcheroo is one you can usually complete on your own and in a short amount of time. The bad news is that, because of the extensive array of models and materials available, it may prove difficult to choose the one style that charms you most. Juxtaposing materials such as porcelain, stainless steel, and forged iron with textures and finishes such as hammered, distressed, and satin produces endless possibilities for product selection.

Having choices is certainly a positive prospect, but it can also be a daunting one. To help you start your search, we've highlighted some of the hottest hardware on the market today—from sleek sophisticates to intricate classics and some fun fobs in between.

Feminine Fobs // Master crafters of America's historic antique hardware, House of Antique Hardware finds inspiration in the belief that period homes were designed and built with unmatched integrity. To restore that integrity and incorporate it into homes today, they have taken the responsibility of meticulously reproducing the workmanship and design details, such as hardware, found in those properties from the past. Perusing its selection of original and authentic hardware, these reproduction glass knobs—both cheerful and charming—stole our heart. Available in an incredible array of difficult-to-locate authentic period colors, these feminine fobs can dress up any decor. House of Antique Hardware, www.houseofantiquehardware.com.

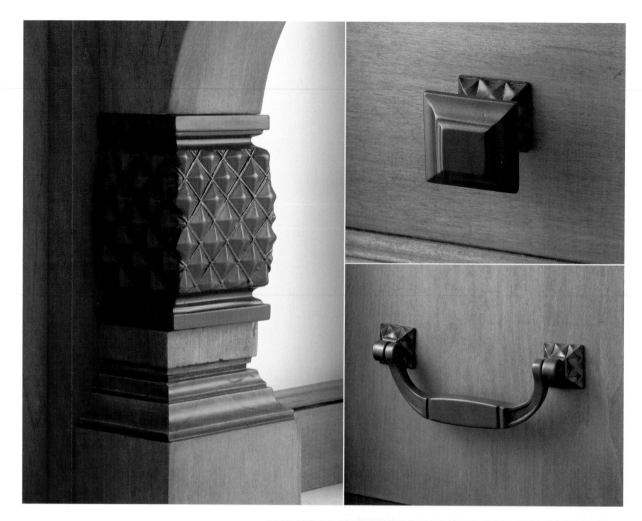

→ Right On Target // If you're aiming for an accent with impact, you'll be right on target with the red and white glass Luster Pimento knob from Sietto. With each and every knob and pull produced one at a time with unmatched craftsmanship, Sietto's handmade glass hardware hits the mark when making over bathroom vanities, furniture pieces, and more. Plus, if the Pimento knob isn't on point with your palette, Sietto also offers custom applications. With more than 100 different glass color options, Sietto can set you up with truly one-of-a-kind cabinet decor. Sietto, www.sietto.com.

← A Tasteful Touch // A symbol of welcome since the Colonial days when it was a popular hostess gift, the pineapple has been popping up in home-decor products ever since. Whether you want to signify a welcoming style or simply have a taste for the exotic, the new Pineapple Decorative Collection from Häfele America Co. is sure to bear fruit in beautifying your bath. Professionally designed exclusively for Häfele, the pineapple hardware tastefully blends with a variety of home designs. The knobs and pulls are also the perfect complement to the rest of the collection, which includes pineapple-inspired onlays and inserts available in both metal and wood. Häfele America Co., www.hafele.com.

← A Double Shift // Part of Rocky Mountain Hardware's Ted Boerner Collection, the Shift series of decorative hardware pulls pull double design duty. Both artistic and rustic in its aesthetic, this piece's appearance only tells half the story. The other half: the Shift style is as sustainable as it is stunning. A first-time collaborator with Rocky Mountain Hardware, Boerner's environmental sensibilities melded well with those at the company, where products contain 90 percent recycled materials, 50 percent of which is postconsumer. Artful and eco-friendly, this pull will have you wanting to pick up an extra Shift or two for your home. Rocky Mountain Hardware, www.rockymountainhardware.com.

→ **Taking Flight //** Nature lovers, rejoice! Like a fabulous art find in a flea market, the finch cabinetry knob from Rocky Mountain Hardware will excite you. The bird series of knobs is another part of the Ted Boerner Collection. (See "A Double Shift," page 37.) An accomplished San Francisco-based furniture designer, Boerner lent his creativity to five new hardware series, including the bird series, and infused his organic sensibilities into the styles. The result: a fun fob that is sure to take flight in any home setting. Rocky Mountain Hardware, www.rockymountainhardware.com.

↑ **Form and Function //** With an incredible amount of hardware know-how gained from more than 40 years of searching the globe for the greatest in home design products, Richelieu Hardware stays on point with product traditions and trends in its extensive selection of decorative hardware. If functionality and ergonomics are first priorities, then form and fashion come in as close seconds. In all of Richelieu's contemporary, classic, and eclectic styles, world-renowned designers combined time-tested craftsmanship with the latest in materials and finishes for one-of-a-kind creations that are sure to shine on your cabinets. Richelieu Hardware, www.richelieu.com.

Destination Design // Drawing on iconic destinations such as the Great Wall of China, Australia's Sydney Opera House, London's Tower Bridge, the ancient Egyptian city of Luxor, Africa's Victoria Falls, and Rome's romantic Trevi Fountain, the new Passport Collection from Top Knobs puts the world at your fingertips. Known for its exceptional kitchen and bath cabinet hardware, Top Knobs mixes culture and craftsmanship with this collection's series of exquisitely shaped knobs, pulls, handles, appliance handles, and other pieces—all of which are offered in a variety of popular finishes. Top Knobs, Inc., www.topknobs.com.

→ Keeping Tabs // If decorative hardware is considered jewelry for cabinetry, then Rocky Mountain Hardware has decided to put a ring on it. A design gem that manages to stand out even among the many stunners in the company's Ted Boerner Collection, the Round Tab pull in high-glitz gold has a sculptural style that is sure to impress. For anyone keeping tabs on the latest trends, the Round Tab pull is one design adornment you won't want to miss. Rocky Mountain Hardware, www.rockymountainhardware.com.

Shining Design

THIS MASTER BATH STARTED OUT as an incredibly outdated space, broken up into two small, difficult-to-navigate rooms. To make the space livable and beautiful, Barry Miller of Simply Baths redesigned the area for these Connecticut homeowners.

To create different zones within the bath, a few walls were removed, and the toilet was placed in a private space with a window. A French door allows natural light to filter through to the rest of the bath, as does the skylight, which is strategically positioned above the tub.

Porcelain tile provides the distinguished look of tumbled marble at a lower cost and with less maintenance. A roomy shower is the ideal place to unwind after a long day, and the tub deck extends into the shower where it can be used as a seat.

The rich cherry cabinetry is the perfect complement to the warm-toned porcelain tile, which leads right up to the luxuriously large soaking tub.

Even though the overall square footage remained the same after the remodel, the space has better lighting and feels much more spacious. The homeowners couldn't be happier about their redone retreat. «

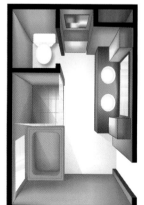

DESIGNER
Barry Miller
Simply Baths, a division of The Brush's End Inc.
37A Padnaram Rd.
Danbury, CT 06811
203.792.2691

SPECIAL FEATURES
Spacious bath with an integrated platform tub and shower

DIMENSIONS
9' x 14'

PRODUCTS USED
Cabinetry: Woodpro, Nottingham, cherry sable finish
Flooring: Porcelain tile, Panaria-Amber Fiorita
Countertops and Tub Deck: Caesarstone, champagne limestone
Sinks: Kohler Caxton
Faucets: Danze Fairmont, brushed nickel
Bathtub: MTI Victoria II
Shower Door: Custom Frameless
Toilet: Kohler Cimmarron
Lights: Norwell Lighting
Drawer Pulls: Tob Knobs

MEMBER OF
SEN DESIGN GROUP

PHOTOGRAPHER: DAVID DADEKIAN

A Suite Retreat

THE OWNERS OF THIS PRINCETON JUNCTION, NEW JERSEY, home wanted to change the style of their bathroom to accommodate something more in line with their discerning tastes. They gave designer John Lang, of Lang's Traditions Kitchen and Bath, and Fran Pappas a simple edict: keep everything white, but stay in tune with the look and design of the rest of the house.

The toughest challenge, Lang said, was removing an old fireplace from the room. Doing this cleared the way to relocate the massive 6-foot tub and created space for a custom shower, complete with tiled columns of Alabastro porcelain and tumbled limestone. The extra space also accommodated an area for a beautiful granite vanity.

The original bathroom had two entrances. Removing one led to a custom-closet renovation that allows accessibility from the bathroom without disturbing anyone who might be sleeping in the bedroom. In keeping with the family's desire to "keep everything white," Jay Rambo cabinetry was finished in a glaze that provided a French country look.

Once the home of an outdated fireplace, this room now offers an inviting warmth that is sure to provide many reasons to spend time in this retreat. «

DESIGNER:
John A. Lang
Lang's Traditions
Kitchen and Bath
9 Summit Square Cntr.
RT 413 & RT 332
Langhorne, PA 19047
215.860.4143
215.860.3920

SPECIAL FEATURES:
Whirlpool tub; custom glass shower door; cabinets to countertops for extra space; multishower body sprays

DIMENSIONS:
15' x 12'

PRODUCTS USED:
Tile: Alabastro porcelain, tumbled limestone
Cabinetry: Jay Rambo
Mirrors: Custom glass
Sink: Kohler
Tub: Kohler
Toilet: Kohler
Shower Door: Easco
Vanity Tops: Granite
Plumbing Supplies: Ondine, Jaclo

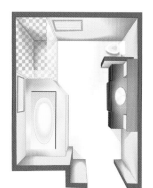

PHOTOGRAPHER: STEVEN PAUL WHITSITT

Grecian Timelessness

When luxuriating in their newly renovated master bath, these homeowners couldn't be happier with the custom features and high-end products used to transform the space. The mastermind behind this design is Phil Bjork of New Jersey-based Kuche+Cucina. With over three decades of design and build experience, Bjork wove the old and the new throughout the space to create a custom look that fits the homeowners' tastes with the amenities that make taking a break from their busy lifestyle a breeze.

When planning the design, Bjrok made sure to include his and her sections with a built-in tub as the focal point. This spacious layout perfectly accommodates two large custom vanities as well as a glass-and-tile shower. The size of the room allows for some bold design elements, with wood paneling and Corinthian columns. The vanities were built for maximum storage without sacrificing style. They are outfitted with undermounted sinks and fine furniture details that include fluted panels on either side of the mirrors.

While Bjork incorporated classical details, he was sure to include all of the modern amenities a modern-day master bath needs. *Learn more about this designer at www.kuche-cucina.com.* «

DESIGNER
Phil Bjork
Kuche+Cucina
489 Route 17 S.
Paramus, NJ 07652
201.261.5221

268 Main St.
Madison, NJ 07940
973.937.6060

ALLIED PROS
Alida Avallone
Avallone Interiors
Wyckoff, NJ, 07481
(P) 201.891.6769
(F) 201.891.6818

SPECIAL FEATURES
His and her sections;
built in tub; wall
paneling; pedestals with
columns and Corinthian
capitals

DIMENSIONS:
16' x 19'

PRODUCTS USED
Cabinetry: Custom wood
Flooring: Tile
Vanity Tops: Marble
Lighting: Chandelier

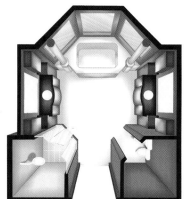

PHOTOGRAPHER: KEN LAUBEN

Soothing Suite

LOCATED IN THE LUSH horse country of Alpharetta, Georgia, just off the Georgia Tech Club private golf course, this 11,000-square-foot home was originally featured as a House of Dreams showhouse in the developing neighborhood. A site to behold in and of itself, the master suite is designed to be a private escape from the hustle and bustle of life. Boasting a bedroom, a morning bar, a private sitting area, and a master bath, the suite invites its residents to rest in the soothing grandeur of the space.

Designed by Bette Raburn, ASID, and Blake Howell, Allied ASID, of The Interior Motive, the master bathroom has a spalike ambiance. A spa tub and large walk-in shower with body sprays invite indulgent soaks or steamy showers. A towel-warming drawer on one side is another appreciated amenity. Raburn and Howell also designed separate his and her vanities to provide residents with ample private prep space. "Her" side includes tall wall cabinets with mullion glass doors and a beauty center. A pullout cushioned seat provides the perfect locale to sit comfortably under the mirror, beneath the bright lights overhead. The well-fashioned retreat is a soothing sanctuary within the comfortable confines of the home. «

DESIGNERS
Bette Raburn, ASID
Blake Howell, Allied ASID
The Interior Motive
6582 Peachtree
Industrial Blvd,
Norcross, GA 30071
770.242.2784

SPECIAL FEATURES
Towel-warming drawer;
separate his and her
vanities; spa tub; and
large walk-in shower

DIMENSIONS
11' x 24'

PRODUCTS USED
Tile: Dal-Tile, natural
stone
Cabinetry: UltraCraft,
cherry, Carnegie
door-style
Mirrors: Custom
Sinks: Kohler Caxton
Tub: Jason Tub
Toilet: Kohler
Shower Door: Custom
frameless
Vanity Top: Granite,
honed
Plumbing Supplies:
Kohler, oil rubbed
bronze
Drawer Pulls: Top Knobs
Towel-Warming Drawer:
Thermador

MEMBER OF
SEN DESIGN GROUP

PHOTOGRAPHER: JOEL SILVERMAN, SILVERMAN PHOTOGRAPHY

Touches of Luxury

THIS BATH IN CAPE COD, MASSACHUSETTS, was a complete remodel that redefined the many fragmented areas of the room and created one spacious, functional layout.

Two separate sinks and two small closets were not very user friendly. To solve the problem, Linda Whitcomb of Village Kitchen & Bath Design opened up the space by removing interior walls and doors and taking out the tub. In its place, she added a superb shower with a multihead function and a walk-in European style entrance to eliminate the closed-in feeling. The bather is now surrounded by massaging streams of water for complete relaxation.

The shower boasts a mixture of large, light-colored ceramic and glass tiles, in conjunction with an acid-washed shower panel to allow for light and privacy. To make room for a spacious his-and-her storage area, Whitcomb redesigned a nearby bedroom. Now the homeowners have a large walk-in closet accessible from the master bathroom.

The room blends European elegance with classic New England style. The new space is more like a spa getaway than a traditional bath, with convenient his-and-her storage and use areas. The underfloor heating system and the towel warmer add even more touches of luxury to this accommodating space. «

DESIGNER
Linda Whitcomb
Village Kitchen
& Bath Design
707 Main St.
Hyannis, MA 02601
508.771.5446

SPECIAL FEATURES
Blending European influence of the shower and heating system with New England traditional styling of the room

DIMENSIONS
13' x 10'

PRODUCTS USED
Cabinetry: Dura Supreme Designer
Flooring: Dal-Tile
Countertops: Granite, Giallo Veneziano
Sinks: American Standard Loft
Faucets: Danze
Wallcovering: C-2 paint
Towel Warmer: Zehnder
Radiant Heating: Warmly Yours

MEMBER OF
SEN DESIGN GROUP

PHOTOGRAPHER: STEVE VIERRA

Revisited Vista

THIS HOME, LOCATED IN SEA PINES PLANTATION RESORT, HILTON HEAD ISLAND, SOUTH CAROLINA, was in need of a bath remodel that had to be as stunning as its views of the Atlantic Ocean. The homeowners wanted a reposeful escape to wash away the day and a space that would accommodate their extended family. To get the renovation in shape, the homeowners called upon Brent Blair of Low Country Kitchen & Bath.

The first challenge was the tub, an undermount-model that had to be fitted precisely within the granite deck. The unlevel floor was another challenge. To accommodate the 18 x 18-inch limestone slabs, the design team had to level the subfloor. To do so, the exterior French door was removed, and the area was raised 2 inches. For an added touch of luxury, a radiant heating system was installed beneath the floor, sure to keep feet warm.

The custom frameless shower enclosure and the Nevada gold granite surfaces give the space the refined upgrade it needed. Undermounted stainless-steel, round lavatory bowls sit in the vanity. To add a bit more custom detailing to the bath, a decorative border of hand-broken mosaic stone adorns the wall. In the end, the design was a perfect complement to the home and to the sweeping seascape beyond it. «

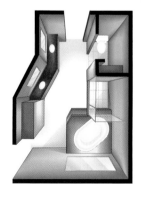

DESIGNER
Brent T. Blair
Low Country
Kitchen & Bath
1 Matthews Dr., Ste. 105
Hilton Head Island, SC 29926
843.689.2124

SPECIAL FEATURES
Designed around many angles; radiant floor heating under limestone; hand-broken mosaic stone

DIMENSIONS
20' x 16'

PRODUCTS USED
Tile: 18 x 18-in. Monaco Light honed limestone; hand-broken mosaic stone border
Cabinetry: Bertch Elan custom
Mirrors: Allied Brass, Waverly Place round tilting
Sinks: Decolav undermount round stainless steel
Toilet: American Standard
Shower Door: Custom frameless, clear glass
Vanity Tops: Granite Nevada Gold
Plumbing Supplies: Danze Sirius
Drawer Pulls: Tob Knobs

MEMBER OF
SEN DESIGN GROUP

PHOTOGRAPHER: STEVEN PAUL WHITSITT

Classic Beauty

To transform this bath in Jarrettsville, Maryland, into the stunning space it is today, Michael Watts CGR of Bel Air Construction utilized an unused bedroom, creating a large master suite.

Chocolate brown walls set the tone for this reposeful space. The custom marble shower provides the perfect escape after a long day. It's equipped with an extensive shower system to massage and relax. The nearby towel warmer keeps linens toasty. The sleek tub sits next to the shower and boasts a built-up custom edge treatment for the marble deck. Both the shower and tub are perfect complements to the timeless design.

Plenty of storage solutions line the wall under the vanity, with all of the cabinetry finished in antique white. The vanity's lighting casts a soft glow, providing the ideal environment for preparing to step out and greet the world. The design also includes a separate toilet area.

Perhaps the most notable feature of the design is the exquisite double-sided fireplace, transforming the space from a bath to a true private oasis. Now these homeowners have a classic design that will last for years to come. «

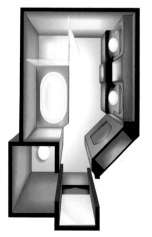

DESIGNER
Michael Watts CGR
Bel Air Construction
1655 Robin Cle.
Forest Hill, MD 21050
888.557.1222

SPECIAL FEATURES
Utilized unused bedroom for master suite

DIMENSIONS
19' x 10'

PRODUCTS USED
Tile: Crema Marfil marble
Cabinetry: Dura Supreme, Sophia antique white, espresso glaze
Mirrors: Custom
Sinks: Kohler
Tub: Kohler
Toilet: Kohler
Shower Door: Custom
Vanity Tops: Crema Marfil marble
Lights: Kichler
Plumbing Supplies: Moen faucets and shower system
Drawer Pulls: Tob Knobs
Towel Sarmer: Zehnder
Fireplace: Montigo
Vent: Fantech
Windows: Pella

MEMBER OF
SEN DESIGN GROUP

PHOTOGRAPHER: DEAN RAY, RAY STUDIOS

Bright Ideas

This bathroom in Naperville, Illinois, was a complete remodel. The space was reconfigured by Nicole M. Weiland of Casa by Charleston to fit the homeowners' exact specifications—they desired a timeless theme with great amenities and a highly functional design.

The big challenge in this space was the lack of light. The original window was tucked in the corner of the room, so the window was enlarged from 2 to 4 feet wide. This also provided a window in better proportion to the space. Can lighting and updated vanity light fixtures also help illuminate the bath.

The homeowners also wanted to implement separate his and her zones. And because they never used their whirlpool tub, they replaced it with a smaller soaker. Now the vanities sit on either side of the corner tub.

Dark sable cabinetry and travertine tile are used throughout the space to provide its classic look. Mosaic tile and glass accents at the vanity and shower areas give the travertine an extra punch. Crisp white plumbing fixtures, creamy quartz countertops, and warm oil-rubbed bronze accents complete the look. Now the whole family can't wait to relax in the new space! «

DESIGNER
Nicole M. Weiland
Casa by Charleston
15 W. Jefferson Ave.
Ste. 103
Naperville, IL 60540
630.718.1440

SPECIAL FEATURES
His and her vanities; travertine tile; enlarged custom shower

DIMENSIONS
14' x 11'

PRODUCTS USED
Tile: Dal-Tile, American Olean
Cabinetry: Bertch Legacy
Mirrors: Custom
Sinks: Decolav
Tub: MTI
Toilet: Kohler
Shower Door: Custom
Vanity Tops: Tigris Sand Silestone
Lights: Murray Feiss
Plumbing Supplies: Price Pfister
Drawer Pulls: Tob Knobs

MEMBER OF
SEN DESIGN GROUP

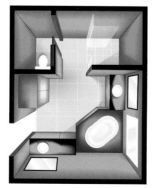

PHOTOGRAPHER: SHERMAN DUNNAM

Curves Ahead

To MAKE THIS BATH more functional, it needed a spacious and design-savvy makeover. The space also needed to accommodate the family, who are married professionals with a daughter in college. To ensure that the remodel would yield fantastic results, the homeowners enlisted designer Rhonda L. Bower of Interior Concepts in Beckley, West Virginia.

Her challenge: to fit a corner whirlpool tub in the space while leaving enough room for a walk-in shower. She not only successfully solved that problem but added a curving glass-block shower wall as well. And with the help and expertise of Bryan Heffernan, owner of Sunset Tile, that design element also was a complete success. The glass-block wall helps to keep the room bright with generous amounts of natural illumination.

The low threshold of the shower adds a pleasing aesthetic, and its easy accessibility will accommodate the homeowners for years to come. The Jacuzzi tub, with its massaging jets and body-contoured design, is the perfect way to relax after a long day. A tiled border runs along the wall, unifying the entire room. «

DESIGNER
Rhonda L. Bower
Interior Concepts
119 2nd St.
Beckley, WV 25801
304.255.6808

SPECIAL FEATURES
Curved glass-block shower wall; custom low-threshold shower with no door and glass block; glass accent tiles and matching CaesarStone vanity top; contemporary fixtures

DIMENSIONS
10' x 13'

PRODUCTS USED
Tile: Dal-Tile
Cabinetry: Woodpro, Lambiere Collection, maple
Sink: Kohler
Tub: Jacuzzi Corner Whirlpool
Toilet: St. Thomas Creations, Palmero, one-piece, elongated
Vanity Tops: CaesarStone, Pacific Reflections
Lights: Ulextra, contemporary brushed-nickel sconces, mirror; recessed can lights, ceiling
Plumbing Supplies: Danze, Bannockburn Collection
Drawer Pulls: Woodpro
Radiant Flooring: Warmly Yours
Glass Block: Dal-Tile

MEMBER OF
SEN DESIGN GROUP

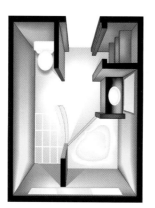

PHOTOGRAPHER: STEVE BRIGHTWELL

Rich Design

WHEN APPROACHING THEIR BATHROOM REMODEL, these urban homeowners knew they were looking for anything but ordinary when it came to outfitting it in their high-rise apartment with city views. Favoring bold design and custom touches, they hired a designer who felt comfortable working with a variety of materials, Phil Bjork of Küche+Cucina. With more than three decades in the business and complete design and fabrication experience, Bjork rose to the challenge of meeting these homeowners' unique requests.

A focal point of the master bath is a mahogany vanity with olive ash burl on the raised panels of the doors and drawers surrounded by a lamb's-tongue trim detail molding. Above the vanity are two diagonal open display cabinets with a mirror between them. The balance of the room features mahogany wainscoting with recessed panels capped with an acanthus chair-rail molding.

The perfect balance between his and her design, the room's vibrant wall coloring and rich materials are offset by elegant gold touches in faucets and trimming. Spacious, so both the husband and wife can use the space at once, the master bath is outfitted with his and her sinks as well as a separate shower and bath.

Learn more about this designer at www.kuche-cucina.com. «

DESIGNER
Phil Bjork
Küche+Cucina
489 Route 17 S.
Paramus, NJ 07652
201.261.5221

268 Main St.
Madison, NJ 07940
973.937.6060

SPECIAL FEATURES
Custom materials including mahogany and marble; custom vanity complete with two diagonal open display cabinets with recessed mirror; recessed paneling wrapping around the room

DIMENSIONS
12' x 14'

PRODUCTS USED
Cabinetry: Custom
Flooring: Marble
Vanity Tops: Marble
Wallcovering: Mahogany wainscoting with recessed panels wrapped with lambs tongue trip; top cap is an acanthus chair rail molding

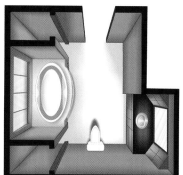

PHOTOGRAPHER: KEN LAUBEN

Luxury Spa

THIS LUXURY HOME in California's Sonoma County, built by D&R Construction, warranted a master bath to fit the serene setting. Designer David Fryn of Northbay Kitchen & Bath helped the clients choose and purchase the materials to create a luxurious master bath that includes a bay window overlooking the wine country.

The expansive area contains an air-jetted tub set into a granite surround by Crema Marfil marble tile. The etched-glass shower has a built-in seat, along with a deluxe shower system complete with a rain showerhead to offer a soothing deluge of water. Separate his and her vanities topped with Costa Esmeralda granite slabs handsomely serve the couple's individual needs. The cabinetry provides plenty of storage space.

Subtle lighting adds to the intimacy and luxury-spa feeling. Recessed halogens provide general illumination, with diffused wall lighting on either side of the vanity mirror. Every detail spells sophistication, from the decorative glass-tile inserts in the Creme Marfil marble floor to the crown molding used throughout the design. The sweeping view of the rolling hills rounds out the pleasure of this master bath. «

DESIGNER
David Frym
Northbay Kitchen & Bath
822 Petaluma Blvd. N.
Petaluma, CA 94952
707.769.1646

SPECIAL FEATURES
Deck-mounted tub with bay window, etched glass shower enclosure

DIMENSIONS
19' x 12'

PRODUCTS USED
Tile: Crema Marfil marble
Cabinetry: Dura Supreme
Mirrors: Custom
Sinks: Kallista
Tub: Bain Ultra Jetted Tub
Toilet: Toto
Shower Door: Custom etched glass
Vanity Tops: Granite
Lights: Seagull Lighting, recessed halogens
Plumbing Supplies: Rohl; Michael Berman
Drawer Pulls: Top Knobs

MEMBER OF
SEN DESIGN GROUP

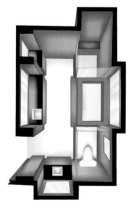

PHOTOGRAPHER: STEVEN PAUL WHITSITT

Steamy Indulgence

THIS BATHROOM IN A HOME located on Town Mountain in Asheville, North Carolina, was a complete remodeling project. The space was gutted, and one wall was extended to accommodate the new steam shower.

Although it was the first total custom-cabinetry project she had ever tackled, April Hand of Benbow & Associates summoned her keen eye for design, jumped right in, and got the project off to a flawless start.

The homeowners requested specific drawer sizes and countertop heights, and they needed plenty of storage space. The designer worked closely with the owner of the house to ensure that everything she and her husband wanted fit perfectly into the space. Robern mirrored medicine cabinets keep everything neatly stored away.

The epitome of tranquility, the new space contains everything the homeowners desired. The water-closet door is custom-made solid walnut, as are all the trim and cabinetry. The custom-built steam shower comfortably fits two, and an Ipé hardwood bench provides a place to relax in the soothing steam. The shower also has a stunning view of the mountains beyond and the city below. In the end, the homeowners couldn't have asked for more! «

DESIGNER
April Hand
Benbow & Associates Inc.
38 Glendale Ave.
Asheville, NC 28803
828.281.2700

SPECIAL FEATURES
Custom-built steam shower for two; ipe hardwood bench in shower

DIMENSIONS
6' x 19'

PRODUCTS USED
Tile: Marble Systems, Metropolitan Stone Collection
Cabinetry: Custom-made of walnut by Benbow & Associates
Mirrors: Robern Medicine Cabinets
Sinks: Kohler
Shower Door: Bullseye Glass
Vanity Top: Corian
Lights: Brilliance, ice sconce
Plumbing Supplies: Hansgrohe
Drawer Pulls: Richelieu
Bench: Custom-made by Benbow & Associates, Ipé

MEMBER OF
SEN DESIGN GROUP

PHOTOGRAPHER: DAVID DETRICK

Smooth Moves

Seeking a more luxurious and refined space for her master bath, this homeowner knew her dream design would require drastic change. So she turned to the trusted designer she had used for her kitchen remodel, Gary A. Lichlyter of Lemont Kitchen & Bath.

Early in the design process, they decided to eliminate the rarely used whirlpool tub to free up valuable floor space. In fact, the new design would require moving every plumbing fixture. The toilet and sinks were transferred across the room to create space for a much larger shower outfitted with a large seat and heavy glass door. Wall-to-wall cabinetry on two sides of the room created plenty of storage and grooming space.

Paneled walls above the vanity add formality and beautifully frame the sconce lighting and matching medicine cabinets. An armoire-style cabinet and matching window seat with drawers are both functional and beautiful. A shallow diagonal corner cabinet was created to house the new LCD TV and additional storage. And a custom, full-length, three-way mirror was hung behind the door.

Behind the delightful design, technology keeps things working and comfortable. A floor-warming system keeps the limestone floors cozy, even on the coldest nights. The resulting room is truly an elegantly appointed master suite. «

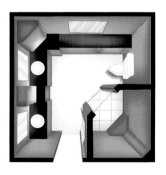

DESIGNERS
Gary A. Lichlyter
Christopher E. Fleming
Lemont Kitchen & Bath, Inc.
106 Stephen St.
Lemont, IL 60439
630.257.8144

SPECIAL FEATURES
Recessed medicine cabinets; large shower with multiple showerheads; furniture-style cabinetry

DIMENSIONS
12' x 12'

PRODUCTS USED
Cabinetry: Shamrock Cabinets
Flooring: Limestone
Vanity Tops: Sahara marble
Sinks: American Standard
Toilet: American Standard
Medicine Cabinets: Robern
Radiant Floor Heat: Warmly Yours

MEMBER OF
SEN DESIGN GROUP

PHOTOGRAPHER: STEVEN PAUL WHITSITT

Reimagined Retreat

INSPIRED BY AN OLD WORLD LOOK with a contemporary touch, these Connecticut homeowners decided to bring their large but inefficiently organized master bath to its full potential. With the help of designer Barry Miller, owner of Simply Baths, the couple redesigned their cramped and outdated bath to maximize luxury, comfort, and space.

The challenges the original space presented were a confining shower stall and a tub and tub deck that took up more than one-third of the room. The homeowners also wanted to fit in two sinks without compromising vanity space. By installing a freestanding tub, Miller was able to enlarge the shower considerably and give it the roomy feel and mood-enhancing light the old shower lacked. The new space easily accommodates a vanity with two vessel sinks, plenty of storage, and a makeup counter. The marble mosaic floor tile and the tile adorning the wall add warmth and a simple elegance to the room.

In addition to the spacious and comfortable aesthetic, the homeowners now enjoy a spalike setting with features such as a steam shower and heated flooring. The new bathroom uses space to its advantage, adding more comforts while creating a fresh, open atmosphere suitable for relaxation. «

DESIGNER
Barry Miller
Simply Baths, a division of The Brush's End
37A Padanaram Rd.
Danbury, CT 06811
866.NuBath1

SPECIAL FEATURES
Curb-free steam shower; radiant heat under tile; remote blower fan for the air tub to reduce noise in the bath

DIMENSIONS
9' x 16'

PRODUCTS USED
Cabinetry: Plain & Fancy Custom Cabinetry
Flooring: AKDO tile
Vanity Tops: AKDO marble tiles in Cream Pearl
Sinks: DECOLAV
Shower Fixtures: JACLO
Sink and Tub Fillers: The Rubinet Faucet Company LaSalle Collection
Tub: MTI Whirlpools Antigua tub
Steam Unit: Mr. Steam
Toilet: Toto Nexus
Radiant Floor Heat: Warmly Yours

MEMBER OF
SEN DESIGN GROUP

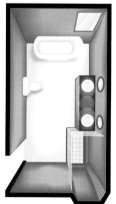

PHOTOGRAPHER: DAVID DADEKIAN

Balcony Bath

To TRANSFORM THIS outdated bath into a spalike retreat, the homeowners called upon Marcelo Dobrauchi of Terranova Construction, K & B Inc. They wanted the space to have a traditional look while exuding a feeling of absolute tranquility. To make it even more unique, the room opens onto a balcony. But above all, the biggest challenge would be to create the feeling of a spa in the small space.

To achieve the desired Zen-inspired ambiance, the designer focused on a shower with multiple showerheads. He also included an exterior sliding door that allows the homeowners to step onto the balcony in the morning. This new addition also floods the space with light. The use of natural stone throughout the bathroom and in the tub makes the space feel even more luxurious.

The custom storage and magazine box next to the toilet adds a unique touch. The completely custom frameless shower enclosure enhances the overall flow of the room, and the large mirrors help the area appear even more spacious. Now the homeowners have a reposeful retreat of their very own, complete with warmed floors to keep their toes toasty and comfortable. «

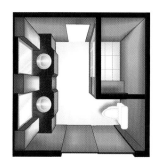

DESIGNER
Marcelo Dobrauchi
Terranova Construction,
K & B Inc.
8453-Q Tyco Rd.
Vienna, VA 22182
703.761.0604

SPECIAL FEATURES
Multiple showerheads;
door-matching
cabinetry; heated floors

DIMENSIONS
11' x 14'

PRODUCTS USED
Tile: Florida Tile
Cabinetry: Bertch Legacy
Vanity Tops: Emperador
Dark marble
Sinks: Kohler
Shower Door: Custom
Toilet: Toto
Plumbing Supplies:
Danze Sheridan
Collection
Lighting: Forecast
Mirrors: Custom frames
with sheet mirrors

MEMBER OF
SEN DESIGN GROUP

PHOTOGRAPHER: JUNE STANICH

Old Is New Again

THIS DECADES-OLD HOME in Springfield, Massachusetts, had been slowly restored over the years, and it was now the bath's turn for a modern update. Interstate Custom Kitchen & Bath, Inc., gutted the room to the studs and completely reframed the shower and tub areas.

Because of the hip roof, the room's configuration presented a small challenge when the project was started. However, special planning and custom cabinetry solved the problem. The dark wood used for the cabinets was the perfect complement to the rest of the home.

The homeowners also wanted to keep the glass-block window, which had previously been boarded up and, therefore, did not allow natural illumination to enter the space. The designer also removed a closet, which opened up the room and allowed for the addition of the walk-in shower. The radiator was also removed and replaced with an alternative warming device: radiant heating, which was installed under the floors.

The designer took future maintenance needs into consideration as well and created access to the whirlpool mechanics with a removable panel. A framed mirror adds to the elegance of the bath, as does the lovely granite whirlpool tub deck. Now this formerly outdated space has the contemporary renovation it deserved. «

DESIGNER
Interstate Custom
Kitchen & Bath, Inc.
558 Chicopee St.
Chicopee, MA 01013
413.532.2727

SPECIAL FEATURES
Accommodation of
existing glass-block
window; custom
cabinetry

DIMENSIONS
9' x 10'

PRODUCTS USED
Tile: Caribe in Dorado
Cabinetry: Christiana
Cabinetry in cherry
wood
Vanity Tops: Emerald
Pearl granite
Sink: Corian
Faucet: ShowHouse by
Moen
Tub: Maax whirlpool
Shower Door: Custom
Toilet: Toto
Radiant Floor: Warmly
Yours
Window: Pella

MEMBER OF
SEN DESIGN GROUP

PHOTOGRAPHER: STEVEN PAUL WHITSITT

Mountain Sanctuary

THIS BEAUTIFUL MASTER BATHROOM in Silverthorne, Colorado, is the perfect retreat after a day on the ski slopes. Designer Amanda Good of Aspen Grove Kitchen & Bath, Inc., worked closely with builder Vasiliy Gansyak to achieve the perfect combination of elegance and rustic mountain character in this new home.

The homeowners now soak their sore muscles in the large Kohler whirlpool tub while enjoying the mountain views. The tub features a custom granite deck. The majestic vista is enhanced by large slate tiles capped with a border of small irregular pieces. The application of dense rock continues in the relaxing steam shower, which has a slate shower surround and custom slate shower pan (not shown). The complementary cabinetry features lightly distressed carriage-black paint. To add visual interest, the center unit is raised and features free-form granite countertops. Venetian Bronze finish on all the Delta fixtures provides the perfect finishing touch to this rustic retreat.

The main challenge in this master bathroom was meeting the schedule, but despite the crunch, no detail was missed. The walls are all faux painted, and each piece of small broken slate was carefully set by hand. The result is stunning and sure to please. Luxury mountain living is at its best here in the Colorado Rocky Mountains. «

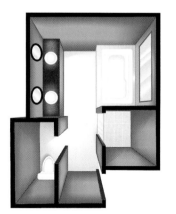

DESIGNER

Amanda Good
Aspen Grove Kitchen &
Bath, Inc.
721 Granite, A1
Frisco, CO 80443
970.468.5393

Vasiliy Gantsyak
D.I.A.N.A. Services, Inc.
970.389.2931

SPECIAL FEATURES
Multilevel vanity top;
free-form granite tub
step, slate mirror frames,
and slate backsplash

DIMENSIONS
14' x 11'

PRODUCTS USED
Cabinetry: Medallion
Cabinetry
Flooring: Slate polished
Vanity Tops: Comet
granite
Backsplash: Slate
Hardware: Emtek
Products
Sink: Kohler
Faucets: Delta
Plumbing Fixtures: Delta
Steam Shower: Delta
Tub: Kohler
Toilet: Kohler

MEMBER OF
SEN DESIGN GROUP

PHOTOGRAPHER: TIMOTHY FAUST

Bathing Beauty

THIS BATH REDESIGN IN RESTON, VIRGINIA, was completely customized to match every desire the homeowner had in mind. A successful businesswoman, she desired a place to wash away the day, and Ricki Weber of Baths by RJ was ready to create the perfect space.

Upon meeting her client, Weber realized the homeowner had created a dwelling in which her exquisite taste was evident in every corner—except in her master bathroom. By studying the design used throughout the house, Weber soon discovered the homeowner's tastes, which included bold and provocative stylings with a large dose of whimsy. The home was filled with interesting pieces, and despite their varying genres, all seemed to complement each other. So the main design challenge was to create an environment that worked well with the existing one without exceeding a reasonable budget.

By devoting ample time and in-depth research to the project, Weber was able to devise the perfect design. The bench and shower step are finished in the the same beautiful stone as the countertop. A custom mirror and mosaic tile shower floor and wall borders are other details that make this daring design a complete success story. Final touches, such as the onyx vessel bowl with the faucet mounted on the mirror, complete this beautiful bath. «

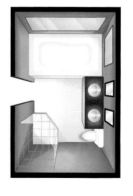

DESIGNER
Ricki Weber
Baths by RJ
10013 Blue Coat Dr.
Fairfax, VA 22030
571.221.3797

SPECIAL FEATURES
Onyx vessel bowl; custom-designed mirror; faucet and light mounted in mirror; rock mosaic on shower floor and wall

DIMENSIONS
8' x 12'

PRODUCTS USED
Flooring: Florida Livingston Gold tile
Cabinetry: Kraftmaid Lindsay with Ginger Glaze on Cherry
Vanity Tops: Absolute Black granite
Sinks: Suneli, Mansi, onyx vessel
Shower Door: Century Glasstec in Satin Nickel
Shower Tile: Island Rocks Mosaics
Plumbing Supplies: Kohler Stillness in brushed nickel
Toilet: Kohler San Raphael
Lighting: Quoizel
Drawer Pulls: Castlewood Sugarstone
Mirrors: Custom
Wall Mosaic: Island Rocks Mosaics

MEMBER OF
SEN DESIGN GROUP

PHOTOGRAPHER: STEVEN PAUL WHITSITT

Warm and Gracious

THIS MASTER BATH was a complete remodel of an owner-built two-story Colonial-style home located on the outskirts of Chapel Hill, North Carolina. The house received a total makeover—including the kitchen, each of the bathrooms, and various other areas—by Pierce Cassedy of Cassedy & Fahrbach Design Partners.

The challenge was updating the style and function of the master bathroom for this professional couple while successfully collaborating with them on design ideas.

There were many notable features that went into this project, and each led up to a final design that could not make the homeowners happier. Case in point: warming tiles feel soothing to feet in the morning when stepping into the space and are perfect after climbing out of a steamy soak in the luxurious tub. The water closet with a bidet is separate from the bathing area to provide comfort and convenience.

To create visual warmth in the space, rich, handcrafted mahogany wood tops complement the furniture-style cabinetry and beautiful mirror frames. A large shower with a curved glass-block wall (not shown) provides a crisp contrast to the cabinets. Now this couple has an exquisite escape to match the rest of their newly updated space. «

DESIGNER
Pierce Cassedy
Cassedy & Fahrbach
Design Partners
P.O. Box 788
Pittsboro, NC 27312
919.542.2578

SPECIAL FEATURES
Furniture-grade vanities with recessed sinks, custom-built mahogany countertops, separate water closet

DIMENSIONS
11' x 16' bathroom;
6' x 9' water closet

PRODUCTS USED
Cabinetry: Elmwood Kitchens
Vanity Tops: Custom; mahogany
Sinks: Porcher
Tub: Americh soaking tub
Toilet: Toto
Plumbing Supplies: Grohe fixtures
Heated Floor: Warmly Yours
Drawer Pulls: Cliffside

MEMBER OF
SEN DESIGN GROUP

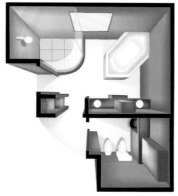

PHOTOGRAPHER: STEVEN PAUL WHITSITT

Soothing Sanctuary

To help these homeowners achieve total comfort so that they can be at their best for career and family, Cook Remodeling designed a private sanctuary to energize, soothe, and renew. Making up the list of must-haves for this Arizona couple: a walk-in shower, a tub, separate walk-in closets, their own laundry, a chandelier, and a private office/library.

This project offers many solutions to relieving stress. The adjacent library is a quiet retreat with French doors that lead to a patio, complete with soothing sounds from a stacked-stone waterfall feature. The glass-block shower floods the space with natural light. Its Danze Rainhead shower fixture offers another means to experience the sensation of nature. Eliciting fond memories even when not in use, an old-fashioned Victorian claw-foot tub is surrounded with bead-board.

"Her" walk-in closet addition has floor-to-ceiling enclosed cabinetry to tuck away clothes and maximize storage. It has an adjacent stacked washer and dryer. The closet is oversize to include their treadmill and space to exercise. The husband enjoys having his own walk-in closet. His expanded bathroom gave the space for a seating bench perfect for stretching and massages. The wife enjoys her personal vanity with ample counter space and flattering illumination. Cook Remodeling's solutions for this couple's needs and lifestyle have made a great space in which they can begin and end each day. «

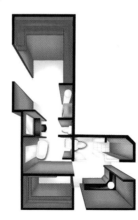

DESIGNER
Cook Remodeling &
Custom Construction, Inc.
1370 W. Los Lagos Vista Ave.
Mesa, AZ 85202
480.491.3077

SPECIAL FEATURES
Walk-in glass-block shower with built-in bench, rainhead shower fixture, and hand-held shower; slipper tub with Victorian hardware and bead-board surround on wall; hidden stacked washer and dryer; fully enclosed walk-in closet that doubles as an exercise room with multilevel chandelier

DIMENSIONS
26' x 40'

PRODUCTS USED
Tile: Dal-Tile
Cabinetry: Dura Supreme
Sink: Kohler, his; Queen Anne pedestal sink, hers
Tub: Parisian slipper tub with claw feet, British telephone faucet
Toilet: Kohler
Shower Door: PPG, glass block in IceScapes
Vanity Tops: Dal-Tile
Lights: Halo recessed lighting
Plumbing Supplies: Danze Rainhead
Flooring: Dal-Tile, baths; Shaw carpet, walk-in closet; Mohawk engineered wood, sitting room
Wall Covering: Dal-Tile, walk-in shower; DuraSupreme beadboard, tub

MEMBER OF
SEN DESIGN GROUP

PHOTOGRAPHER: CHRIS BASSETT OF BASSETT PHOTOGRAPHIC, INC., WWW.BASSETTPHOTOGRAPHIC.COM

Elegant Touches

THIS MASTER BATH IN DALTON, GEORGIA, was a full remodel. In fact, the entire space was taken down to the studs and subfloor. After the demolition was done, G. Kyle Dinsmore, CKD, of Georgia Kitchen and Bath Design took the design to the next level.

Reshaping the room was the biggest challenge. The toilet was relocated from sharing a space with the shower to having its own secluded area. This created the interesting challenge of finding a place for it. The solution: remove a linen closet door and frame and place the toilet in the closet. A knee wall was added for privacy. The shower was expanded, and a teak bench replaced the old toilet.

Both vanity sinks were moved, and the outdated 1970s cultured-marble tub replaced by a classic double-soaker cast-iron claw-foot model. Tile from Spain adds pattern to the floor, and matching tile with a glass border is used in the shower. The designer applied a Venetian plaster technique to the walls, and his addition of Crème of Bordeaux granite adds another touch of luxury to the space. «

DESIGNER
G. Kyle Dinsmore, CKD
Georgia Kitchen and
Bath Design
222 N. Hamilton St.
Dalton, GA
706.278.3374

SPECIAL FEATURES
Shower stall; claw-foot
tub; overall space
management within the
footprint of the room

DIMENSIONS
10' x 15'

PRODUCTS USED
Cabinets: Bertch custom,
Centurion in chestnut
with heavy black glaze
Faucets: Mico, Moen
Tub: Elizabethan Classic
claw foot with double
slipper
Tile: Porcelain

MEMBER OF
SEN DESIGN GROUP

PHOTOGRAPHER: KYLE DINSMORE

Elegant Escape

ALEX RODRIGUEZ OF PRIORITY ONE CONTRACTORS CORPORATION met with these Washington, D.C., homeowners after they had interviewed multiple companies to complete their bathroom renovation. After the clients decided that his design team was exactly who they wanted, Rodriguez immediately set to work planning this bath's major facelift.

Because the homeowners had their eye on this neighborhood for a long time, it was quite a special project. Not only did they finally have the location of their dreams, but now they would have a spalike escape to match their every desire.

The team used undercabinet power strips and light fixtures to supplement the room's natural light. A drop-in tub and a granite deck provide a luxurious look in the bath, and two vanity cabinets on either side allow for plenty of storage. A walk-in shower offers a pulsating hydro-message to wash away all of the day's stress.

No details were overlooked during this elaborate process. An underlayment system, designed specifically for ceramic tile, serves as a waterproofing membrane to ensure that moisture doesn't accumulate beneath the tile. The outcome was an elegant escape, ideal for these new homeowners. «

DESIGNER

Alex Rodriguez
Priority One
Contractors Corporation
7528 Diplomat Dr.
Ste. 201
Manassas, VA 20109
703.330.7993

SPECIAL FEATURES

Drop-in tub with granite deck; two vanity cabinets with matching granite tops; walk-in shower

DIMENSIONS

13' x 19'

PRODUCTS USED

Tile: Dal-Tile
Flooring: Crystal, custom
Mirrors: Custom
Sinks: Kohler
Tub: Kohler
Toilet: Kohler
Shower Door: Custom
Vanity Tops: Granite, tub deck and surround
Lights: Kichler
Drawer Pulls: Tob Knobs
Bidet: Kohler

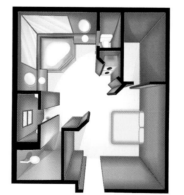

PHOTOGRAPHER: R.C. KREIDER

Majestic Makeover

AFTER ROOMSCAPES INC. successfully remodeled their kitchen to culinary perfection, this Mission Viejo, California, couple decided that their bathroom was also deserving of a major face-lift in preparation for visits from their grown children and grandchildren. With Roomscapes designer Deborah Nassetta, CKD, CBD, CID, at the helm, the transformation began.

The bathroom had to be gutted for a full remodel, as the original space provided several challenges and inspired many changes. It had unattractive floating soffits with fluorescent lights, and the vaulted ceiling was too high and had a large exposed beam. Lowering the ceiling, Nassetta added a center coffer with indirect LED lighting and a chandelier, which added a formal grace and elegance to the bath design.

The original bathtub was too small and had a lot of empty deck space, so Nassetta selected a larger, much deeper tub and extended the platform into the shower to create a bench (shower not shown). The new shower was enlarged and includes a rain shower and traditional showerhead, as well as a hand shower. The frameless glass enclosure evokes a feeling of openness and exposes the beautiful stone shower walls and brushed-nickel fittings. Bespoke with beauty, this rehabbed bath is guaranteed to pamper through the generations. «

DESIGNER
Deborah Nassetta, CKD, CBD, CID
Roomscapes Inc.
23811 Aliso Creek Rd.
Ste. 139
Laguna Niguel, CA 92677
949.448.9627

SPECIAL FEATURES
Double vanities; glass makeup table; burl wood inlays; coffered ceiling

DIMENSIONS
14' x 19'

PRODUCTS USED
Cabinetry: Woodmode Grand Tour in cherry
Tile: Marble mosaic and Alabastrino travertine
Vanity Tops: Emperador light polished marble and glass
Sinks: Kohler Memoirs
Tub: Bain Ultra Azur Whirlpool
Shower Door: Custom frameless
Toilet: Caroma dual flush
Lights: Wilshire Tango sconces
Hardware: Schaub Montcalm Collection
Mirrors: Custom with beveled edge
Flooring: Emperador light marble and Alabastrino travertine

MEMBER OF
SEN DESIGN GROUP

PHOTOGRAPHER: LARRY FALKE

Overhaul Oasis

SET AMID A PANORAMIC HILL-COUNTRY LANDSCAPE, this down-to-earth Austin, Texas, home celebrates kicked-back comfort at its finest. The original master bath, however, felt miles apart from the nature-inspired nuances so evident throughout the rest of this abode. With just two small corner windows, it lacked the interior-meets-exterior air the homeowners so cherished. To create a cohesive design, they dialed up Mark Lind, senior project designer at CG&S Design-Build.

After he completely gutted the room, Lind swapped the existing spec-home finishes and plumbing fixtures for more appropriate finishes in travertine, slate, and mahogany paneling. He combined the tub and shower into a single wet area behind a frameless glass panel. The solid travertine tub deck coordinates with the travertine at the vanity top and with the wall and floor tile as well. The distinctive slate tile on the tub skirt is repeated in the shower's horizontal shampoo niche.

The focal point: a 12-foot-wide, view-maximizing window above the vanity that opens up the bathroom to the great outdoors. Mahogany cabinets at the vanity harmonize with the wood paneling at the toilet compartment, which features horizontal panels separated by ½-inch reveals and a sliding mahogany door on a hidden overhead track. The final product? An enlightened bath that nods to nature via an assembly of earthy elements. «

DESIGNER
Mark Lind
CG&S Design-Build
402 Corral Ln.
Austin, TX 78745
512.444.1580

SPECIAL FEATURES
Two-person shower area with wall-mounted sprays and ceiling-mounted rain heads; curvilinear whirlpool tub filled by Kohler faucet mounted flush with the ceiling and featuring built-in reading light; individual mirrors above sinks supported on cables to allow for view of surrounding terrain

DIMENSIONS
8' x 16'

PRODUCTS USED
Cabinetry: Amazonia Custom Cabinetry
Flooring: Travertine
Vanity Tops: Moe Freid Marble and Granite
Sinks: Kohler
Faucets: Kohler
Tub: Price Pfister
Toilet: Kohler
Wallcovering: Slate

PHOTOGRAPHER: GREG HURSLEY PHOTOGRAPHY

DESIGNER

Guillaume Gentet
Décor by Guillaume
Gentet
139 Fulton St., Ste. 417
New York, NY 10038
212.571.1040

SPECIAL FEATURES

Walker Zanger Searock
Blue rectangular
tile hung vertically;
extensive application
of Carrara marble; deep
soaking tub; custom
vanities with built-in
bench

DIMENSIONS

10'3" x 19'3"

PRODUCTS USED

Cabinetry: Custom
decorator with Benjamin
Moore white paint in
high-gloss finish
Flooring: Artistic Tile
Carrara marble
Vanity Tops: Carrara
marble
Sinks: Kohler
Plumbing Fixtures:
Waterworks
Tub: Napoli from Victoria
Albert
Shower Door:
Toilet: Toto
Lighting: Leucos
Medicine Cabinet:
Waterworks
Hardware: Kraft
Side Table: Plexicraft
Trash Can: Plexicraft
Wallcovering: Walker
Zanger Searock Blue
rectangular tile

Brilliant in Blue

WHILE THIS OLD ENGLISH-STYLE home's façade is
traditional to a T, its interior is a prismatic collection of
color-infused glass vessels and other decorative accents and
accessories. The home gained its multichromatic theme
thanks to an ongoing transformation that was the result of
creative teamwork between the homeowners and designer
Guillaume Gentet of Décor by Guillaume Gentet.

The color continues in the master bedroom, which is
even adorned with a vivid painting custom made by the man
of the house. While the owners wanted to make a splash in
their master bathroom as well, they also wanted to infuse
the space with calming clarity.

A study in spalike simplicity, Gentet washed the walls
in Walker Zanger Searock Blue rectangular tile hung
vertically. The Carrara marble tile flooring extends up the
wall a few feet to meet the tile. A deep white soaking tub
and frameless glass-enclosed shower with
custom marble bench further the clean
and clear aesthetic. The vanities, also in
white, were custom made. Gentet even
designed a stool that was part of the
cabinet but unfolds as a bench.

Brilliant in blue and white, this spa-
worthy space is a true calm corner in
this vibrant home. *Learn more about this
designer at www.guillaumegentet.com.* «

PHOTOGRAPHER: ALEX KROKE

Back in Business

THE TRUST IS a mid-century-built structure in downtown Charlotte, North Carolina, that was recently converted from a lending institution to luxury condos. The homes are a clever fusion of past meets present. But the rich, deep finishes in this master bath, combined with the lack of natural light, made it too dark. To solve this problem, Kaity Slaughter of DCI Home Resource put her design mettle to work.

First, she replaced the vanity with a wall-hung model to lighten the look. The dark-toned cabinets and trim finish are offset with light and neutral tiles in this space.

The custom-enclosed shower and whirlpool bathtub provide an exquisite experience, with multiple Kohler body sprays, dual showerheads, and glass doors. These smart design moves are sure to please any homeowners. And the luxurious vanity wall adorned with textured custom tiles and sleek vertical mirrors hugged by contemporary sconces on each side effectively fast-forward the room into the 21st century.

When all is said and done, the room has been successfully transitioned into an oasis of luxury and light. «

DESIGNER
Kaity Slaughter
Mary Beth Hartgrove
DCI Home Resource
1300 South Blvd., Ste. C
Charlotte, NC 28203
704.926.6000

SPECIAL FEATURES
Custom enclosed shower and whirlpool tub; suspended double-bowl vanity with cabinetry in an espresso quarter-sawn oak finish; luxurious vanity wall with textured custom tile

DIMENSIONS
18' x 17'

PRODUCTS USED
Cabinetry: Pedini Integra Moro
Tile: Crossville Tile and Stone of Charlotte
Vanity Tops: Marble
Sinks: Kohler Ladena
Plumbing Fixtures: Kohler
Tub: Kohler
Hardware: Richelieu

MEMBER OF
SEN DESIGN GROUP

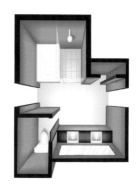

Redefined Elegance

THIS LARGE MASTER BATH was awash in design challenges for Jim Meloy, CKD, of Kitchen & Bath Concepts in Roswell, Georgia. His task: to utilize the dimensions and unique shape of the existing room while incorporating the homeowners' specific requests. After Meloy presented the clients with several configurations, they picked the one that best met their lifestyle needs, and he went to work.

To maximize floor space, the designer moved an entry door and relocated the water closet to an area that had been linen storage. Angling the walls allowed for a spacious shower with a built-in seat, multiple showerheads, and body sprays. A frameless shower door and glass side panels heighten the sense of spaciousness. Meloy also swapped the outmoded bathtub for a jetted version complete with an air-bath system. Framing the tub, travertine tiles with pewter accents gleam in the light-filled area.

Meloy also installed travertine tiles in the shower, on the tub surround, and on the floor, which is heated by a radiant warming system. Extra-tall cabinets flank the shower; one contains a towel warming drawer. Double vanities feature even more stowaway spots.

All told, the new bath is a custom-tailored retreat that overflows with sophistication and functionality. «

DESIGNER
Jim Meloy, CKD
Kitchen & Bath Concepts
11444 Alpharetta Hwy.
Roswell, GA 30076
770.442.9845

SPECIAL FEATURES
Body sprays and multiple showerheads; floor warming system; towel warming drawer; custom green paint

DIMENSIONS
20' x 10'

PRODUCTS USED
Cabinetry: Holiday Kitchens
Tile: Travertine
Vanity Tops: Corian Antarctica
Sinks: Corian
Plumbing Fixtures: Santec
Tub: MTI
Shower Door: Custom
Toilet: Kohler
Hardware: Top Knobs
Mirrors: Custom by Holiday Kitchens
Towel Warmer: Thermador drawer
Heating: Warmly Yours radiant floor

MEMBER OF
SEN DESIGN GROUP

Inspired Renewal

THIS CONNECTICUT COUPLE transformed their outdated, cramped master bathroom into an orderly retreat. By maximizing the existing space and smoothing the transition between features, designers Barry Miller and Diane Miner of Simply Baths helped the homeowners achieve a space that is as functional as it is fashionable.

The original shower was too closed in, and the tub was squeezed between it and a wall. The goal was for an updated, contemporary look with a larger shower. The new one is larger and enhanced with glass walls. It boasts an attractive tower that contains body jets and a showerhead. Its one-piece design not only looks sleek but also allows for simple installation. The shower integrates seamlessly with the new tub—a tile mosaic borders the shower and tub surround. A storage ledge runs continuously across the tub and shower as well.

Two glass sinks and a glass countertop add a modern edge to the room, while soft shades of tan combine with the brown glass mosaic backsplash and shower floor to add depth without overpowering or darkening the room.

The new bathroom is both practical and stylish—the perfect place to gear up for the day or leave it behind. «

DESIGNER
Barry Miller and
Diane Miner
Simply Baths, a division
of The Brush's End, Inc.
37A Padanaram Rd.
Danbury, CT 06811
203.792.2691

SPECIAL FEATURES
Removal of walls around
tub to allow for a large
shower and integrated
tub deck

DIMENSIONS
10' x 14'

PRODUCTS USED
Flooring: AKDO Fibra
Canvas
Vanity Tops: Clear glass
Sinks: Glass
Shower Door: ½-inch
frameless clear glass
Shower Floor: AKDO
Mojave Blend glass oval
Shower Walls: AKDO
Crema Pearl marble
Shower Faucet: Grohe
Aqua Tower
Tub: Jason AirMasseur
with LED
Chromatherapy Light
Tub Faucet: American
Standard Tub Filler in
chrome
Toilet: Toto Nexus
Ventilation: Fantech
remote vent fan
Heating: Warmly Yours
radiant floor heat
Wall Accent Tile: AKDO
Natural Blend polished
marble mosaic accent
tile

MEMBER OF
SEN DESIGN GROUP

PHOTOGRAPHER: DAVID DADEKIAN

To New Heights

SITUATED IN A 1970s-era home overlooking Oneonta, New York, the original bathroom was anything but user friendly. The homeowners, a family of four with two active preteens, were desperate for an elegant and relaxing room that would be functional for everyday use. They tasked Michael Stockin, CKD, of Kuntriset Kitchens & Baths Design Center with the total remodel.

Stockin's dual hurdles: the low ceilings—just over 6 feet on the outside wall—and elongated layout. The husband is over 6 feet tall, so Stockin's challenge was to create a room that would comfortably accommodate him as well as the rest of the family. First, he sited the shower against the inside-corner wall, positioning the fixtures at just the right height. He then set the tub under a large opaque-glass corner window, which allows for maximum light while providing a measure of privacy. Stockin also installed a glass wall between the tub deck and the shower to flood the shower with sunshine.

Lighted full-height mirrors channel a lofty feel, and recessed glass shelves neatly house sundries. Cabinets flanking a granite-topped bump-out are another pretty place to corral clutter. All in all, this was a happy ending to an involved job. «

DESIGNER
Michael Stockin, CKD
Kuntriset Kitchens &
Baths Design Ctr.
5127 State Hwy. 12
Norwich, NY 13815
607.336.4197

SPECIAL FEATURES
Custom tile shower; drop-in Whirlpool tub; granite vanity top highlighted with turn post

DIMENSIONS
10' x 14'

PRODUCTS USED
Cabinetry: Brookhaven with Edgemont recessed door style
Tile: Florim ceramic Navajo Series
Vanity Tops: Crystal Gold granite
Sinks: Deca undermount porcelain bowls
Faucets: Kohler Devenshire Series
Tub: Jason Whirlpool
Shower Door: Coastal
Toilet: Kohler Welworth Series
Lights: Task Lighting recessed cans
Hardware: Top Knobs
Mirrors: Custom

MEMBER OF
SEN DESIGN GROUP

PHOTOGRAPHER: STEVEN PAUL WHITSITT

Relax to the Max

BETWEEN THEIR TWO kids and work, these busy homeowners are always on the go. They wanted the ultimate luxury shower experience so that they could finally fit a little relaxation into their schedule. They also wanted to ensure privacy so that they could share the space with the children. Incorporating all of these desires into such a small space was the daunting task of Marcelo Dobrauchi from Terranova Construction, K&B Inc.

To achieve the first goal, Dobrauchi designed a grand steam shower with six showerheads for maximum comfort. He added a three-part tankless water-heating system to ensure an unending flow of hot water while saving energy. Each showerhead can be controlled independently to mix and adjust temperature for custom bathing. Finally, Dobrauchi created a recessed towel-warmer niche inside the shower so that incredibly cozy towels are always ready.

He completed the second goal by employing a frosted-glass enclosure that maintains privacy without detracting from the pleasing aesthetics. Dobrauchi also allocated a separate room for the toilet.

Aesthetically, Dobrauchi incorporated varied tile types, patterns, and materials. With this artist's touch, the bathroom is now the relaxing retreat these homeowners craved. «

DESIGNER
Marcelo Dobrauchi
Terranova Construction,
K&B Inc.
8453-Q Tyco Rd.
Vienna, VA 22182
703.761.0604

SPECIAL FEATURES
Multiexperience shower,
including steam shower
and towel warmer inside
shower

DIMENSIONS
9' x 9' main bath;
3' x 5' water closet

PRODUCTS USED
Cabinetry: Bertch Legacy
Tile: Florida Tile
Vanity Tops: Cabernet
Brown marble and
Antigua granite
Sinks: Kohler
Plumbing Fixtures:
Kohler
Shower Door: Custom
³/₈-inch glass
Toilet: Toto
Lights: Forecast Bath
Mirrors: Custom tiled
frame with sheet mirrors

MEMBER OF
SEN DESIGN GROUP

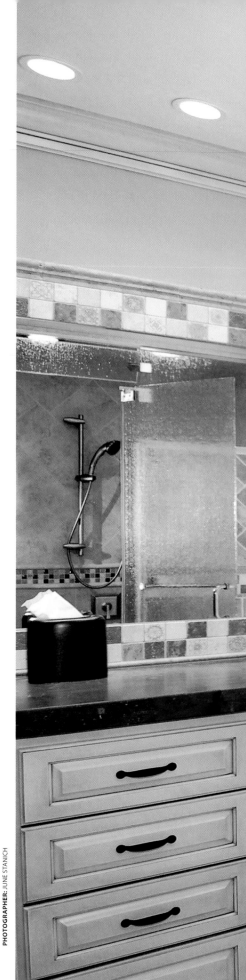

PHOTOGRAPHER: JUNE STANICH

Personality Plus

THIS RAMBLING CALIFORNIA RESIDENCE in the Napa Valley is the epitome of beauty. However, its owners were less than impressed with the bland master bathroom. So they turned to Catherine Shackford of Northbay Kitchen & Bath for a redesign.

To create a master bath with five-star-hotel flair, Shackford added drawer-top cabinets and a valance over the vanities. Custom knotty-alder cabinets complete with rounded corners dress up the design to the nth degree.

Shackford integrated an etched-glass oak tree motif for the shower door and toilet area. Slate floor tile and wainscoting add other elements that make the room special. For exhilarating escapes at the end of an exhausting day or a fete-filled night, the Bain Ultra tub with air jets and the steam-unit-equipped shower round out the pampering room.

Thanks to Shackford's thoughtfully conceived new bath, her clients are now proud owners of a space that's the antithesis of everyday design. «

DESIGNER
Catherine Shackford
Northbay Kitchen & Bath
1916 Yajome St.
Napa, CA 94559
707.224.1020

SPECIAL FEATURES
Knotty alder distressed cabinetry with rounded corners; Bain Ultra bathtub with air jets; steam unit installed in shower

DIMENSIONS
19' x 10' tub and shower area;
9' x 6' vanity area

PRODUCTS USED
Cabinetry: Encore custom in knotty alder
Tile: Jeffrey Court Sedona slate and Alpine Rustic slate
Vanity Tops: Caesarstone
Sinks: Toto
Faucets: Rohl polished nickel with crystal levers
Tub: Bain Ultra
Shower Door: Northbay Kitchen & Bath design
Toilet: Toto
Hardware: Top Knobs
Mirrors: Custom

MEMBER OF
SEN DESIGN GROUP

Eyesore No More

NOTHING SHORT OF A FULL BATHROOM GUT and remodel would do for this family of five in Sutton, Massachusetts. Despite the many quality and style updates required, the biggest challenge facing designer Mariette Barsoum, CKD, and Heidi Marika-Perez of Divine Kitchens was to make the space appear much larger than it actually is. First, they removed half the wall separating the shower from the rest of the room. Next went the old framed shower door, replaced with a custom frameless glass model that extends to the half wall. With the area opened, light now pours into it, creating the illusion of a larger room.

The design team then unified the space by overlaying the entire bathroom with a large horizontal tile that supports the grander aesthetic. And they integrated colored glass tiles into the shower floor and the niche. They chose a low-profile toilet and designed a contemporary vanity. Made of dark-finish mahogany, frosted glass, and a wall-mounted cabinet, the vanity appears to float off the wall.

Other updates included replacing the baseboard heater with radiant flooring and installing luxuries such as a towel warmer. In the end, the design team transformed an unsightly bathroom into a chic, modern space that the whole family—and guests—can enjoy. «

DESIGNER
Mariette Barsoum, CKD
Heidi Marika-Perez
Divine Kitchens
40 Lyman St.
Westborough, MA 01581
508.366.5670

SPECIAL FEATURES
Floor-to-ceiling tile all around the room; glass-tile inserts in the shower; shower with half wall; frameless shower door with glass panel; floating cabinet

DIMENSIONS
10' x 5'

PRODUCTS USED
Tile: Daltile
Cabinetry: Prevo Cabinetry
Vanity Tops: Carrara Marble
Sink: Whitehaus Collection
Plumbing Fixtures: Whitehaus Collection
Shower Door: Wayside Glass
Toilet: Toto
Hardware: Top Knobs
Mirrors: Custom
Towel Warmer: Runtal Towel Warmer

MEMBER OF
SEN DESIGN GROUP

PHOTOGRAPHER: LORETTA BERARDINELLI

Asian-Inspired Oasis

As busy executives with children, this Hillsborough, New Jersey, couple dreamt of decompressing at the end of the day in a spalike retreat. The only problem? Their house had no such space. Lucky for them, some extra square footage in the attic presented the perfect solution. To transform this bonus zone into an in-home haven, the homeowners hired Ray Ferraro of All Trades Contracting. For a pleasing symmetry in the multi-angled space, the designer developed an intricate balance of color and light. He also tiled the tub deck, finishing the edge with an upside-down piece of molding—a resourceful and eye-catching touch. An over-the-tub skylight floods the room in natural illumination.

Other bliss-inducing elements include glass-tile inserts on the floor and shower wall, vessel sinks, an oversized shower with body sprays, and a matching dressing area complete with assorted custom built-in cabinets. Ferraro also included ample storage for toiletries and other grooming-related items. The heated floors are a blessing when a chill is in the air.

And in a fortuitous twist, during his initial survey of the attic, Ferraro found more space than he expected. So he created a Zen-inspired meditation room next to the new bath. Definitely a setup that's double the pleasure! «

DESIGNER
Ray Ferraro
All Trades Contracting
1335 Rt. 31 South
Annandale, NJ 08801
908.713.1584

SPECIAL FEATURES
His and her vessel sinks; heated floor; glass-tile insert on floor and shower wall; air-whirlpool tub; square body sprays and hand shower with square showerhead

DIMENSIONS
12' x 13'

PRODUCTS USED
Cabinetry: Holiday Kitchens Coffee Bean on cherry
Tile: Daltile, Murry
Vanity Tops: Granite Surfaces
Sinks: Ronbow
Plumbing Fixtures: Danze Parma Collection
Tub: Jason Air-Whirlpool
Shower Door: Advanced
Toilet: Toto
Lights: Norwell
Hardware: Top Knobs
Mirrors: Custom

MEMBER OF
SEN DESIGN GROUP

PHOTOGRAPHER: P.M. STUDIOS

Lofty Luxury

WITH ITS BREATHTAKING VISTAS of the capital city and a nearby lake, this Westlake Hills, Texas, home is the epitome of tranquility. The master bath, however, didn't capitalize on the hilltop vantage point, and the owners longed for a luxe retreat where they could soak away their cares. To change that, they called on Julia Dworschack and Steve Wauson of Steve Wauson's Custom Homes of Austin.

The big idea—placing the tub in a loft above the bath—was also the biggest challenge. The solution? The designers, along with architect Mark Canada + Associates, built the shower on the main level to create a comfy place for getting clean and saved the loft for bathing at night. Elegant stone stairs and wainscot lead to the loft, with windows on both sides raised high enough to afford some privacy as well as stunning treetop views.

Three different finishes adorn the travertine floor. The vertical surfaces are polished; the floors and stair treads have a brushed, rustic finish; and small pieces of tumbled stone compose the shower floor. The elegant vanity boasts a single glass vessel with wall-mounted faucets and spout. Now the homeowners can take full advantage of their hilltop haven and bask in the sky-high views any time, day or night. «

DESIGNER
Julia Dworschack and
Steve Wauson
Steve Wauson's Custom
Homes of Austin
5505 Wagon Train Rd.
Austin, TX 78749
512.924.1776

ARCHITECT
Mark Canada + Associates
5013 Trail West Dr.
Austin, TX 78735
512.358.7070

SPECIAL FEATURES
Lofted tub; travertine
floor; glass vessel sink

DIMENSIONS
7' x 12' (loft)

PRODUCTS USED
Tile: Vintage Mexican
travertine stone;
Iridescent Sandstone
from Oceanside Glass
Tiles (wainscot detail)
Cabinetry: Wood by Olin
Fife
Mirrors: Binswanger
Glass
Tub: BainUltra Naos
Thermomasseur
Toilet: Kohler
Shower Door, partition:
Frameless
Vanity Top: Jerusalem
limestone
Lights: Access Lighting
(vanity); Quorum
Lighting (upper sconces)
Plumbing Supplies:
Grohe (shower faucets);
Kohler (vanity, tub
faucets, fixtures)

A Soothing Sanctuary

DESIRING A NEW MASTER BATHROOM for their house built in the 1970s, these Ellsworth, Kansas, homeowners visited the Bartel Kitchen & Bath showroom. The minute they laid eyes on Bartel's newly added bathroom display, they knew that this masterful design was the one for them. To reproduce that stunning look, they consulted with LeWayne Bartel, who created a personalized bath that exceeded all of their expectations.

The stained and glazed hickory is appealing and warm. The vessel sink and glass-tile backsplash set against the brown granite adds more warmth. Storage for sundries and shelves for books flank the toilet, while soft contemporary lighting above and to the sides of the vanity mirror illuminates grooming tasks.

Pure bliss to behold and use, the walk-in shower's corner seat and shower panel and sprays are some of the client's favorite features. Finishing touches include handy drawer organizers for bathroom goods inside the Blumotion drawers and slide-out doors.

Now when the owners come home from the lake, the races, or a day at work, they find comfort and relaxation in this unexpected retreat. *Learn more about this designer at www.bartelkitchenandbath.com.* «

DESIGNER
LeWayne Bartel
Bartel Kitchen & Bath
211 N. Main St.
Buhler, KS 67522
620.543.6767

SPECIAL FEATURES
Cultured marble shower; glass-vessel sink on granite vanity top; glass-tile backsplash; private corner nook for storage and toilet

DIMENSIONS
14' x 19'6" main bathroom
6'6" x 12'6" cut-out

PRODUCTS USED
Cabinetry: Bridgewood Custom Cabinetry in hickory with cherry mahogany stain and brown glaze
Faucet: Kohler vanity
Shower: Onyx
Lighting: SATCO vanity

MEMBER OF
SEN DESIGN GROUP

Innovative Angles

FACED WITH A BORING PALETTE and an underused whirlpool tub, the owners of this Naperville, Illinois, master bath knew that it was time for a remodel. With all of the design challenges that lay before them, the homeowners were overwhelmed. But after hearing a proposed solution from their designer, Jessica A. Todd of Casa by Charleston, the owners knew that they'd have their dream room after all. Todd based her plan on an innovative use of angles, which is evident in this outside-of-the-box design scheme. An angled tub deck helps enlarge the shower space, while the angled entry and frameless enclosure add aesthetic interest. Two recessed niches and a shower seat lend functionality to the room's flair. Todd continued the angled theme by crafting a custom his and her vanity area featuring a large central linen cabinet.

To complete the look, the designer installed cool-blue tile to contrast with the warm-cherry cabinets. The vanity area sports a custom tiled-mirror treatment with floating light fixtures to reflect the room's soothing colors and light. Chrome plumbing and accessories add sparkle. With its carefully crafted concept, Charleston delivered a design that met and exceeded the homeowners' expectations. *Learn more about this designer at www.casabelladesigncenter.com.* «

DESIGNER
Jessica A. Todd
Casa by Charleston
15 W. Jefferson, Ste. 103
Naperville, IL 60540
630.718.1440

SPECIAL FEATURES
Angled tub placement; waterfall; framed mosaic-tile insert; angled custom cabinetry; layout; tile-framed mirrors

DIMENSIONS
11' x 15'

PRODUCTS USED
Tile: Alfa Ceramiche Nepal Sanjani with accents
Cabinetry: Ultracraft Destiny in Shaker Wide Cherry
Mirrors: Custom frameless installation
Sinks: Kohler Caxton undermount
Tub: MTI Whirlpool
Toilet: Kohler Cimarron
Shower Door: Custom frameless enclosure
Vanity Tops: Atlantic Black granite
Lights: Ginger Surface Collection
Plumbing Supplies: Danze Parmaline in chrome
Drawer Pulls: Dekkor in chrome
Other: Zehnder towel radiator

MEMBER OF
SEN DESIGN GROUP

PHOTOGRAPHER: SHERMAN DUNHAM

Sun-Soaked Retreat

THEIR KIDS GROWN AND OUT OF THE HOME, this Chester, New Jersey, couple opted to simplify their life via a domestic downsizing. The master bathroom, though, was one important component on which they did not want to skimp. Devotees of entertaining, the husband and wife keep a very busy calendar and, as such, dreamed of a quiet place to rinse away the day. Envisioning a space replete with luxe appointments, they called on Diane Zehnbauer of Zehnbauer's Kitchen, Bath & More to grant their every wish.

Zehnbauer's biggest test was figuring out how to make the new bathroom function properly for two people without sacrificing an ounce of style. Beyond that, she needed a roomy shower sans doors in the relatively tight space.

To acquire the surplus square footage she needed while fashioning a usable layout, the designer removed the existing his and her closets and replaced them with a walk-in closet from the bedroom. The enlarged windows flanking the tub invoke an at-one-with-nature feel—an element the lady of the house says she absolutely adores.

The fact is, both homeowners are head over heels in awe of their sun-soaked retreat and can't imagine it looking or feeling any other way. «

DESIGNER
Diane Zehnbauer
Zehnbauer's Kitchen,
Bath & More
180 Gold Mine Rd.
Flanders, NJ 07836
973.448.9003

SPECIAL FEATURES
Open shower with no
doors or glass

DIMENSIONS
9' x 10'

PRODUCTS USED
Tile: Tumbled marble
Cabinetry: Woodpro
vanity and shaker door
with medium stain
Tub: Maax
Toilet: Toto
Vanity Tops: Moccachino
marble
Plumbing Supplies:
Kohler, Danze shower
fixture
Floor Heating: Warmly
Yours
Closets: Closet Plus in
walnut

MEMBER OF
SEN DESIGN GROUP

PHOTOGRAPHER: RON ZEHNBAUER

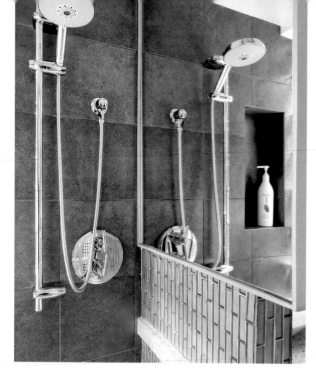

Clearly Cool

DESIGNER
Mark Lind
CG&S Design-Build
402 Corral Ln.
Austin, TX 78745
512.444.1580

SPECIAL FEATURES
All natural light from exterior walls constructed primarily of glass block and a clerestory window above; custom cast-concrete countertop with recycled glass components; shower and toilet compartments screened by central vanity "boomerang" countertop and mirror; Five Star green building rating

DIMENSIONS
11'2" x 11'5"

PRODUCTS USED
Cabinetry: QSI Custom Cabinets of stained walnut and clear-coated MDF
Tile: Porcelain for floor; Pietra Jurassica mosaic stone for shower floor; Walker Zanger Equador Iridescent for vanity
Vanity Top: Venice Art and Terrazo
Sinks: Kohler
Plumbing Fixtures: Grohe
Toilet: Kohler
Lighting: Mouette
Hardware: Ginger
Mirrors: Custom aluminum framing, medicine cabinets by Eric Spille; mirrors by Anchor Ventana

THIS AUSTIN, TEXAS, COUPLE with a collection of midcentury Modern art and furniture decided to renovate their 1950s ranch-style home. There wasn't room for a new master bedroom, bath, and closet within the existing footprint, so an addition was required. The only issue was that the existing house's exterior walls and roof were made entirely of concrete. Mark Lind of CG&S Design-Build had the solution: an all-glass bathroom with a broad, flat roof overlapping the original roof, but raised higher to allow for a bank of clerestory windows.

In the center of the new master bath, a freestanding, boomerang-shaped vanity has a cast-concrete and glass countertop that stands against a green glass-tiled wall with a large rectangular mirror above it. The shower and toilet compartments are tucked away behind this central element, providing privacy. A "flying-wing" fluorescent light fixture suspended from the ceiling fills the space.

The glass-block window had to shield the occupants from outside viewing, yet admit adequate natural light. After an exhaustive testing of various samples, the glass block chosen was the same one used on the house in the 1950s! With their glass bathroom made real using both innovative and throwback materials, these homeowners love their clearly cool addition. *Learn more about this designer at www.cgsdb.com.* «

PHOTOGRAPHER: THOMAS MCCONNELL

Five-Star Elegance

THESE SOUTH-OF-BOSTON HOMEOWNERS wanted to do something for themselves now that their children were off to college. They disliked their bath's closed-in shower stall, oversize tub deck, and lack of style. So they hired Catherine Follett and Ed Spooner of Renovisions, Inc., to transform the space into an elegant, upscale oasis.

The new design called for a freestanding whirlpool tub, with curved panels for easy access to the tub components, and a one-piece Crema Marfil marble tub deck. The adjacent generously sized shower was well appointed with marble tile, a corner seat, and built-in shampoo cubbies, all surrounded by a ⅜-inch-thick frameless glass enclosure.

Large porcelain tiles in a herringbone pattern set a neutral stage to showcase the beaded burgundy cherry vanities with matching mirrors and the tower with Victorian glass. The ogee-edge detail on the Crema Marfil marble countertops, backsplashes, sink cutouts, tub deck, and shower curb further add to the elegance. The pièce de résistance, however, is the faucet and cabinet hardware—Swarovski cut crystals and antique brass. All add to the homeowners' feeling of being bathed in luxury.

Learn more about this designer at www. renovisionsinc.com. «

DESIGNER
Catherine M. Follett
Renovisions, inc.
150 Broadway
Hanover, MA 02339
781.826.0559

SPECIAL FEATURES
Freestanding spa tub with custom curved wood removable panels to access components; ogee edges inside and outside of marble countertops; Swarovski crystals on faucets, tub filler, hand-held showerhead and valve, accessories, and cabinetry hardware; custom built-in cubbies with shelves in matching cherry wood and marble

DIMENSIONS
15' x 21'

PRODUCTS USED
Cabinetry: Dura Supreme Cherry
Tile: Crossville porcelain
Vanity Tops: Crema Marfil marble with ogee edges
Sinks: Kohler
Plumbing Fixtures: WaterMark Design LaFleur collection with Swarovski crystals
Tub: Jacuzzi Salon Spa Whirlpool
Shower Door: Custom frameless glass
Toilet: Kohler Portrait
Lights: WaterMark Design Double Sconce in antique brass, recessed
Hardware: WaterMark Design Swarovski crystal knobs
Mirrors: Dura Supreme cherry framed
Other: Victorian glass in tower doors

MEMBER OF
SEN DESIGN GROUP

PHOTOGRAPHER: DLR PHOTOGRAPHY

Heart of Telluride

WHEN THESE AUSTIN, TEXAS, HOMEOWNERS first came to Telluride, Colorado, they were captivated by its one-of-a-kind beauty. Fifteen years later they decided to purchase a building downtown on Main Street, remodel it, and turn it into a high-end rental that they named "Heart of Telluride." They envisioned a soft mountain feel with neutral colors and a contemporary aesthetic where visitors could relax and unwind after a day of skiing or hiking.

The first challenge for designer Kari Demond of KLM Interiors was to preserve the views and openness from the large, arched windows while maintaining privacy. So she complemented full-length drapes with café curtains on the lower half of the window that can close without obscuring the gorgeous mountain vistas.

A dominant design feature is the see-through fireplace, which adds a warm glow and provides a connection to the bedroom. Also, the antique beveled-glass panels in the doors leading to the bedroom are unexpected and full of personality. Wall colors vary; one wall is finished in a polished Venetian plaster. The sumptuous, full-length drapes soften the hard bathroom surfaces. *Learn more about this project at www.heartoftelluride.com.* «

DESIGNER
Kari Demond
KLM Interiors
4704 Island Cove
Austin, TX 78731
512.458.8081

ARCHITECT
Lynn Taylor Lohr
3115 N.E. 36th Ave.
Portland, OR 97212
503.281.5787

SPECIAL FEATURES
Deep whirlpool bath;
fireplace; Main Street
and mountain views

DIMENSIONS
10'5" x 17'6"

PRODUCTS USED
Cabinetry: Premium alder
with dark cherry finish
Tile: Ann Sacks stacked
Cappadocia White Linen
for floor
Vanity Tops: Black River
granite
Sinks: Kohler Caxton in
biscuit
Plumbing Fixtures:
Kohler Forte in brushed
nickel for sink, shower,
and lavatory handles;
Kohler Revival in
brushed nickel for tub
Tub: Aquatic Serenity XI
in biscuit
Toilet: Kohler Cimarron,
elongated with Brevia
seat and cover in biscuit
Lighting: Antique
crystal chandelier, John
Saladino wall sconces
Hardware: Kohler Forte
Mirrors: Custom by
Chuck's Glass
Draperies: Fabric by
Nancy Corzine, Montauk
Stone 100 percent linen
Doors: Custom premium
alder wood in dark cherry
stain with two antique
beveled glass windows

PHOTOGRAPHER: THOMAS MCCONNELL

Stylized Dream Bath

WHEN SELECTING A CONTRACTOR to renovate their vacation home bath, these owners sought a designer who would go beyond the expected by adding an artistic touch. They found this perfect fusion of function and form within designer Guillaume Gentet, of Décor by Guillaume Gentet.

Once the bath was completely gutted, Gentet set to work adding his unique mark through a series of custom touches that transformed everyday bath staples to vibrant focal points. These included custom-designed, white-lacquered cabinets with white solid-surface vanity tops; a freestanding Duravit tub; RH hardware; Kohler sinks and faucets; and Farrow and Ball wallpaper and paint.

Seamless in its design, you would never know by looking at it that one of the biggest challenges in this bath revamp was the custom cabinetry. The curved detail of the drawer fronts and custom handles adds a stylish flair.

To complete the feel of luxury, final touches included radiant heating in the floors, a Toto bidet toilet equipped with a radio, and glassware sourced from Denmark. *Learn more about this designer at www.guillaumegentet.com.* «

DESIGNER
Guillaume Gentet
Décor by Guillaume Gentet
139 Fulton St., Ste. 417
New York, NY 10038
212.571.1040

SPECIAL FEATURES
Custom-designed, white-lacquered cabinets; Farrow and Ball wallpaper and paint; radiant heating in the floors; bidet toilet equipped with radio

DIMENSIONS
8'6" x 11'

PRODUCTS USED
Cabinetry: Custom designed, white lacquered
Flooring: Tiles from Marrakesh, distributed by Artesana Interiors; radiant heating
Vanity Tops: Custom white solid-surface material
Sinks: Kohler with stainless-steel faucets
Tub: Duravit free-standing tub
Shower: Kohler showerhead, custom glass shower doors
Toilet: Toto, bidet toilet equipped with radio
Hardware: Gracious Home cabinetry, RH hardware
Mirrors: Gaston
Wallcovering: Farrow and Ball wallpaper and paint

PHOTOGRAPHER: ALEX KROKE

Detailed Design

WHEN THIS FAMILY of five decided to undertake a two-story addition to their home in Sutton, Massachusetts, the owners knew a new master bathroom was a must. While they were accustomed to sharing a single-sink vanity and tub/shower combo, they had a much more spa-themed setup in mind.

Their wish list was specific: a soaking tub, a separate walk-in shower for two, and a double vanity with lots of storage. But that list of features grew by one after hiring designers Mariette Barsoum, CKD, and Heidi Marika-Perez of Divine Kitchens, who made the well-received suggestion of incorporating a double-sided fireplace.

The designers placed the tub in front of windows for enjoying garden views. They designed a soffit in the oversize shower to install the rain showerhead at a height for optimum relaxation. Privacy was created in the toilet area without enclosing it by keeping the plumbing wall open on the sides to emit light.

The overall palette—white contrasted by rich cabinetry and a pop of color—and the fun elements—panels surrounding the vanity mirrors—contribute to the uniquely detailed design. The effect is a spa-worthy space reflective of the owners' personalities: hip, modern, and warm. *Learn more about these designers at www.divinekitchens.com.* «

DESIGNER
Mariette Barsoum, CKD, and Heidi Marika-Perez
Divine Kitchens
40 Lyman St.
Westborough, MA 01581
508.366.5670

180 Linden St.
Wellesley, MA 02481
781.489.9090

SPECIAL FEATURES
See-through fireplace; oversize walk-in shower; chandelier; decorative wall panels

DIMENSIONS
15' x 15'

PRODUCTS USED
Cabinetry: DuraSupreme
Flooring: Daltile Kimona Silk tile in White Orchid
Vanity Tops: IceStone in Sage Green with eased edges
Sinks: Toto
Plumbing Fixtures: Graff Atria Collection in Steelnox finish
Tub: Jason International Forma Soaking Tub
Shower Door: Custom
Toilet: Toto Aquia dual flush
Lighting: Glass chandelier, Tech Lighting pendants
Hardware: Top Knobs
Mirrors: Custom
Backsplash: Daltile Polaris, Daltile Egyptian Glass Peridot Fusion blend
Accessories: Ginger & Kimbal & Young magnifying mirror, 3form panels

MEMBER OF
SEN DESIGN GROUP

PHOTOGRAPHER: LORETTA BERARDINELLI

Built from Scratch

WHEN IT WAS TIME for these empty nesters to retire, they gave up vacation homes in Arizona and Montana and headed to their waterfront dream home on Lake Wylie in South Carolina. Unfortunately, they had to rebuild after the original house burned to the ground.

Having lived in their home for a while before the fire, they had the unique opportunity of finding out what worked for them and what didn't. But they found that they loved their home as it was and decided to make only minor improvements. They kept the same overall design and finishes of the original home, which showcased their personal style and exuded a comfortable elegance.

Then to help them restore—and tweak—their master bathroom, they called on designer Elizabeth Beyers of DCI Home Resource. Notable features in their new room include custom two-tiered vanities, matching columns that contain the lighting and electrical outlets, a curved panel on the tub, and a curved cabinet in the water closet. As a finishing touch, the window casing and room crown molding was faux finished to match the cabinetry finish for a cohesive look throughout the master bath suite.

With their new home risen from the ashes, these homeowners are enjoying its renewed beauty. *Learn more about this designer at www.dcihomeresource.com.* «

DESIGNER
Elizabeth Beyers
DCI Home Resource
1300 South Blvd., Ste. C
Charlotte, NC 28203
704.926.6000

SPECIAL FEATURES
Custom multilevel vanities; columns that match cabinetry; custom curved tub panel and vanity fronts

DIMENSIONS
12' x 22'

PRODUCTS USED
Cabinetry: Quality Custom Cabinetry
Flooring: Crema Marfil marble tile
Vanity Tops: Honed Crema Marfil marble
Sinks: Kohler Linea undermount
Plumbing Fixtures: Grohe Geneva Collection
Tub: Kohler
Lighting: Murray Feiss wall sconces on columns
Hardware: Jeffrey Alexander Collection

MEMBER OF
SEN DESIGN GROUP

PHOTOGRAPHER: STEPHEN YOUNG

From Past to Present

For this Methuen, Massachusetts, young professional and her mother, their bathroom was stuck in the 1950s. While the black and pink tiles were in pristine condition, they weren't the only things sporting the rosy hue. The tub, toilet, and wall sink were also pink. Other features dating the space included the metal medicine cabinet with fluorescent side lights and a side outlet that was so old it would not accept polarized plugs.

For an updated bathroom, they asked Jennifer Lemoine of Taylor & Stevens Cabinetry to apply her 12-plus years of experience in home remodeling to revamping their space. Aside from updating and upgrading the overall design, Lemoine's job—and biggest challenge—was reworking the floor plan to include both a large shower with seating and a seated vanity area in the small, narrow bathroom. The new shower now makes a splash with its multiple faucets and rain head.

With their pink tile a thing of the past (replaced by stunning Hirsch blue stained-glass tile) these homeowners are sure to love their newly refreshed bathroom today and for many more tomorrows. *Learn more about this designer at www.taylorandstevens.com.* «

DESIGNER
Jennifer Lemoine
Taylor & Stevens
Cabinetry
1 Industrial Park Dr.
Pelham, NH 03076
603.880.2022

SPECIAL FEATURES
Custom oversize shower with rain head and hand-held showerhead as well as a bench seat; private seated vanity area; Hirsch blue stained glass tile

DIMENSIONS
7' x 12'6"

PRODUCTS USED
Cabinetry: DuraSupreme Sophia door with antique white finish and espresso glaze
Flooring: Daltile Windrift beige
Vanity Tops: Blue Eyes granite
Plumbing Fixtures: Kohler Memoirs Classic
Shower Door: Lawrence Plate & Glass frosted glass
Toilet: Kohler Cimmeron
Backsplash: Hirsch blue stained glass

MEMBER OF
SEN DESIGN GROUP

Style Meets Function

LOCATED IN PICTURESQUE VIENNA, VIRGINIA, this home was crying out for a master-bath remodel. To create a luxurious retreat for these empty-nesters, Marcelo Dobrauchi with Terranova Construction, Kitchen and Bath, Inc., gutted the space, removing walls, moving plumbing, constructing a new commode room, and redesigning the entrance to the master bedroom.

Dobrauchi's biggest challenge was relocating the toilet in the middle of the space to a separate compartment within the room. Cathedral ceilings, which the homeowners wanted to maintain, complicated the issue. Dobrauchi's solution was a daring diagonal move, locating the toilet closer to the master bedroom. This strategic move caused its fair share of difficulties, and the plumbing proved challenging. Though the project manager was doubtful at first, the plumber succeeded by running the lines in a rather complicated but successful manner.

The successful move also centered the window behind the tub, which balances an asymmetrical arrangement of space. The result is a fresh, updated master bathroom with a toilet discreetly hidden in its new location. *Learn more about this designer at www.terranovackb.com.* «

DESIGNERS
Marcelo Dobrauchi,
Kirsten Ederer
Terranova Construction,
Kitchen and Bath, Inc.
8453-Q Tyco Rd.
Vienna, VA 22182
703.761.0604

SPECIAL FEATURES
Capped custom
shower enclosure;
multiple showerheads;
apothecary cabinets
on individual vanities;
bumped-out sinks;
freestanding slipper tub;
radiant-heat flooring;
commode room;
cathedral ceiling

DIMENSIONS
11'6" x 13'

PRODUCTS USED
Cabinetry: Aristocraft
Manchester door in
cherry with Cognac
finish
Flooring: Conestoga
Tile Medieranea
Vatican Gallery DaVinci
terracotta
Vanity Tops: Vyara Gold
granite by Marblex
Sinks: Kohler Kelston
Plumbing Fixtures:
Kohler Kelston
Lighting: Restoration
Hardware

MEMBER OF
SEN DESIGN GROUP

PHOTOGRAPHER: JUNE STANICH

Classically Refined

LOCATED IN WOODBURY, NEW YORK, this soothing bath is the result of a complete remodel by Fara Boico of Classic Kitchen & Bath Center. Originally, the room was a large, poorly designed space with a huge platform tub against the back wall, a configuration that took up nearly one-third of the room's available square footage. The bathroom was also very cold.

To correct these issues, Boico moved the tub to make more efficient use of the room and free up space for his and her vanities. She also added linen cabinets complete with a surplus of storage—a much-needed feature that was previously lacking in the room. Installing under-floor radiant heat improved the room's comfort level.

At the client's request, Boico created two separate toilet areas flanking the entrance to the bath, one including a bidet as well. Boico also installed a large steam shower with a seat, corner shampoo shelves, and grab bars for safety. Glass-tile mosaic accents and a radius wall above the whirlpool, with a custom hand-painted mural, provide the finishing touches on this delightful master bath remodel. *Learn more about this designer at www.classick.com.* «

DESIGNER
Fara Boico
Classic Kitchen & Bath Center
1062 Northern Blvd.
Roslyn, NY 11577
516.621.7700

SPECIAL FEATURES
Handpainted mural on curved wall; glass mosaic accents, his and her vanities and toilet rooms; radiant heat; steam shower; air bath/whirlpool combination tub

DIMENSIONS
16' x 17'

PRODUCTS USED
Cabinetry: Custom with raised cherry wood panels in Colonial Cherry with black glaze
Flooring: Polished porcelain
Vanity Tops: Copper Sunset Zodiaq
Sinks: Kohler undermount
Plumbing Fixtures: Hansgrohe
Tub: Bain Ultra air bath/whirlpool combination
Shower Door: Custom frameless enclosure with clear-glass and brushed-nickel trim
Toilet: Toto
Wallcovering: Serena Marfil tile

MEMBER OF
SEN DESIGN GROUP

Comfortable at Any Age

DESIGNER

Chris Dreith, CMKBD
The Home
Improvements Group,
Inc.
440 Main St.
Woodland, CA 95695
530.666.5061

SPECIAL FEATURES

Curbless shower fully
covered with solid
surface; Shoji doors with
encapsulated washable
facings; towel radiator
for warming towels near
shower room entrance

DIMENSIONS

12'9" x 17'

PRODUCTS USED

Cabinetry: The
Hampshire Co.
Flooring: Tile
Vanity Tops: Hi-Macs
solid-surface materials
Sinks: St. Thomas
Creations
Plumbing Fixtures: Danze
Toilet and Bidet:
American Standard
Lighting: Hubbarton
Forge, Task Lighting
Hardware: Anne at
Home, L.W. Designs
Mirrors: Jerdon custom
hinged
Backsplash: Tile
Towel Warmer: Zehnder
America
Ventilation: Fantech
Shoji Door: Cherry Tree
Design
Radiant Heating: Warmly
Yours

MEMBER OF

SEN DESIGN GROUP

THIS CALIFORNIA RESIDENCE is home to retired
professionals. Designer Chris Dreith, CMKBD, of the
Home Improvements Group, Inc., combined two hall baths
to create one space that would accommodate the owners'
current and future needs. A large curbless shower provides
clearance for potential wheelchair use, and the shower floor
and floor tiles are slip resistant. Shower grab bars and a
corner shower seat offer additional assistance.

To address storage issues, Dreith incorporated a tall
cabinet near the shower, a niche behind the hinged mirror,
a built-in magazine rack, a towel nook near the bidet, shoe
storage with pullout drawers, a pullout under-sink container,
recessed soap and shampoo storage, various drawers, and tilt-
out drawer fronts. Heated floors, a heated towel radiator, and
exterior tankless water heaters add comfort. The bathroom
also boasts Hi-Macs easy-to-clean solid surfaces.

Aesthetically, nature-inspired colors, a
sliding Shoji screen, and replicated Shoji-
style swing doors complement the Asian-
inspired theme throughout the residence.
Cherry cabinets with a black stain match
the antique Chinese chair in the master
bedroom. Dual-pane vinyl windows and a
Solatube above the vanity flood the space
with ambient lighting. «

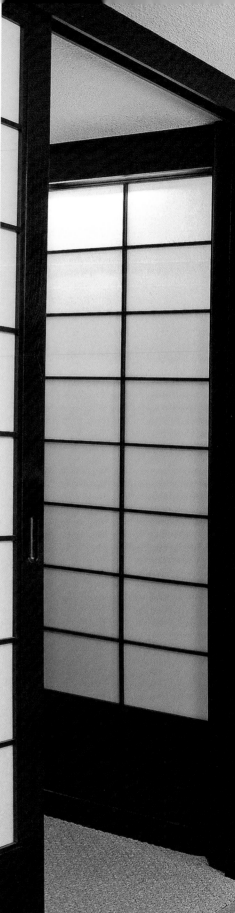

PHOTOGRAPHER: IZZY SCHWARTZ PHOTOGRAPHY

Five-Star Style

AFTER 20 YEARS IN THEIR HOME, this Redding, Connecticut, couple was anxious to exchange their tired, 80s-style master bath for an elegant retreat boasting modern conveniences. Because they were less than fond of the existing space—one that featured a white palette complemented by a red tile border surrounding the tub and shower—the couple desired a radical transformation.

To bring their dreams to reality, they worked collaboratively with Barry Miller and his staff at Simply Baths. Miller immediately set about imbuing the room with an elegant, updated look. He topped the floor, tub deck, and shower with a mosaic Honey Onyx border. Honey Onyx vessel sinks (not shown) and Ubatuba granite complete the embellished decor, while a skylight floods the space with natural light and a warm feel. A large whirlpool tub invites the couple to relax and unwind, and the recessed LCD TV serves up entertainment. When time doesn't allow for an indulgent soak, a two-person shower with eight body jets is equally luxurious.

The bathroom also features ample storage, complete with three closets, three medicine cabinets, and various display niches. Now these homeowners are delighted when they set foot into their newly transformed five-star master bathroom retreat. *Learn more about this designer at www.simplybaths.com.* «

DESIGNER
Barry Miller
Simply Baths
37A Padanaram Rd.
Danbury, CT 06811
203.792.2691

SPECIAL FEATURES
Honey Onyx tile topping the floor, tub deck, and shower; Honey Onyx vessel sinks; Ubatuba granite; inset LCD TV; shower with eight body jets

DIMENSIONS
9' x 14'

PRODUCTS USED
Cabinetry: Woodpro
Flooring: Daltile Honey Onyx
Vanity Tops: Ubatuba granite
Plumbing Fixtures: Danze
Tub: Jacuzzi Elara
Shower Door: Custom frameless
Toilet: Toto Nexus
Backsplash: Daltile Honey Onyx mosaic
Medicine Cabinet: Robern
Radiant Floor: Warmly Yours

MEMBER OF
SEN DESIGN GROUP

PHOTOGRAPHER: DAVID DADEKIAN

Art Lovers' Haven

Nestled in Denver's Cherry Creek area, this open-concept loft is home to two empty nesters who have logged extensive travel miles. As an artist and professed art aficionados, they also possess a large and diverse collection. To showcase it, their interior designer crafted wall spaces and various architectural niches to display specific works of art. Structural columns, which can often create a challenge, were occasionally built out to accommodate a wall sconce, creating an arresting architectural feature. To make the bathroom just as customized, they called on Tamar T. Chang of Thurston Kitchen and Bath.

Though they offered stunning views, the windows made it challenging for Chang to incorporate ample storage. So Chang sought to highlight the view and have the vistas reflected in the dark glass cabinets. Because space was at a premium, every angle had to boast proficient storage. A Pedini shelf with an up-and-down light highlights three-dimensional art objects. Various other Pedini shelves in the powder room create an appealing display. The shelves highlight sculptural pieces as well as framed art mounted below the shelves. Double wall-hung vanities, a large tub deck, and soaring ceilings round out this dramatic art lovers' haven. *Learn more about this designer at www.kitchensofcolorado.com.* «

DESIGNER
Tamar T. Chang
Pedini Colorado/
Thurston Kitchen and
Bath
2930 E. Sixth Ave.
Denver, CO 80206
303.302.0013

SPECIAL FEATURES
Double wall-hung
vanities; glass cabinets
with motion lights;
dressing area; bar (not
shown)

DIMENSIONS
13'11" x 25'4"

PRODUCTS USED
Cabinetry: Pedini Integra
in Silver and Glass finish
Flooring: Tile
Vanity Tops: Granite for
face, quartz for top
Sinks: Integrated with
vanity top
Hardware: Pedini
Mirrors: Custom

PHOTOGRAPHER: WARREN A. JORDEN

A Fresh Approach

SITUATED IN A 1960S MID-RISE BUILDING, the original bathroom was small and crowded. It was also dated. When considering a redesign, the homeowners envisioned an updated bathroom that would feel spacious; radiate a fresh, modern aesthetic; and improve available storage. To bring these dreams to fruition, they called on Jim Wallen, CKD, ASID of Uncommon Spaces, Inc., the same designer who had remodeled their kitchen.

To open the bathroom, Wallen removed the solid partition separating the water closet and cabinetry. To give the space a fresh look, he incorporated bird's-eye maple cabinetry complete with a lighting soffit, panels behind the water closet, and columns encasing the row of medicine cabinets. The designer also lowered the shower pan, removed the shower curb, and incorporated custom panels in clear tempered glass. These efforts made the shower appear larger, while integrating it seamlessly within the room. Blue pearl granite countertops and multicolored glass mosaic tiles add more discriminating details. The remodeled space now functions as a well-appointed master bathroom that no longer pays homage to its original '60s-era design. «

DESIGNER
Jim Wallen, CKD, ASID
Uncommon Spaces, Inc.
1633 Broadway, Ste. C
Oakland, CA 94612
510.834.8400

SPECIAL FEATURES
Bird's-eye maple cabinetry; blue pearl granite and multicolored glass mosaic tile accents; task-angled outlets inside medicine cabinet; step-down shower

DIMENSIONS
9'6" x 5'

PRODUCTS USED
Cabinetry: Hallmark Cabinetry, Inc.
Vanity Tops: Blue pearl granite
Sink: Kohler
Faucet: KWC
Shower Door: Custom panels, clear tempered glass
Showerhead: KWC
Toilet: Toto
Cabinet Pulls: Ginger
Medicine Cabinets: Robern
Lighting: Recessed, Juno Lighting Systems
Ceramic and Tile: Castelvetra, Gemme Series in Agala
Plumbing Fixtures: KWC
Exhaust System: Panasonic
Humidisat: Fantech

MEMBER OF
SEN DESIGN GROUP

PHOTOGRAPHER: STEVEN PAUL WHITSITT

Spacious Retreat

SITUATED IN VILLANOVA, PENNSYLVANIA, this 1980s home lacked charm and architectural detail. To bring these elements into the master suite while creating a bright, spacious retreat, the homeowner called on David Stimmel of Stimmel Consulting Group, Inc.

After demolishing the existing bath and closet, the team created one new open space, complete with built-in storage. This compensated for the lost closet and allowed the client, an on-air television personality, to display his tie collection. The redesigned bath features a recessed paneled ceiling with applied moldings. The panels complement the tub deck and vanity, while infusing the room with the ambiance of a library minus the stuffiness—one of the client's requests. The ceiling is coffered in the center area. Chesapeake by Benjamin Moore is the color of the cabinets and blends them with the surrounding honey onyx tiles. When paired with natural light and lighting fixtures, the variation of color within the tiles is dramatic. To create this effect, a tile designer hand-sorted the tiles so that the color ranges would complement each other. A frameless glass shower enclosure furthers the open feeling. The completed design now boasts a sophisticated escape with the perfect blend of finishing details.

Learn more about this designer at www.stimmeldesign.com. «

DESIGNER
David Stimmel
Stimmel Consulting
Group, Inc.
855 Lewis Ln.
Ambler, PA 19002
215.542.0772

TILE DESIGNER
Leslie Moretti
610.717.8393

SPECIAL FEATURES
Built-in closet unit;
recessed paneled ceiling
with applied moldings;
coffer structure; honey
onyx tiles

DIMENSIONS
19'3" x 10'8"

PRODUCTS USED
Cabinetry: Custom by
Stimmel Consulting
Group
Flooring: Honey
onyx tiles by Marble
Concepts, Philadelphia
Vanity Tops: Honey onyx
slab by Marble Concepts,
Philadelphia
Sinks: Kohler
Plumbing Fixtures:
Kohler
Tub: Kohler

PHOTOGRAPHER: CHARLES MEACHAM

Serene Comfort

DESIGNED BY RAY FERRARO OF ALL TRADES CONTRACTING, this inviting bath is a serene retreat that beckons the homeowners to relax and soak in a little indulgence. The result of a complete remodel, it originally had little natural light due to poor space planning. To open and brighten the room, Ferraro replaced the existing tub and its enclosure with a freestanding model.

Ferraro also installed classic bead-board wainscoting and created his and her prep spaces. Hers features a sit-down makeup vanity, and his boasts ample storage for towels and other necessities. The designer further created a sense of openness by constructing a shower surround featuring two half walls topped with glass. Within the shower, he installed a built-in seat. The shower base features oversize floor tiles with marble inserts to complement the marble countertops. The finished bathroom is now a functional, welcoming atmosphere where the two content homeowners can experience a bit of tranquility while indulging in a soothing soak.

Learn more about this designer at www.AllTradesContracting.com. «

DESIGNER
Ray Ferraro
All Trades Contracting
1335 Rt. 31 South
Annandale, NJ 08801
908.713.1584

SPECIAL FEATURES
Freestanding tub; large shower with seat; bead-board; inset marble on floor

DIMENSIONS
15'6" x 12'

PRODUCTS USED
Cabinetry: WoodPro, cherry, black glaze
Flooring: DAL Salerno
Vanity Tops: Marble
Sinks: Kohler
Faucets: Moen
Plumbing Fixtures: Moen
Tub: Elizabethan Classics
Shower Door: Advanced
Toilet: American Standard
Lighting: Murray Feis
Mirrors: WoodPro

MEMBER OF
SEN DESIGN GROUP

PHOTOGRAPHER: PM STUDIOS

Bel Air Bath

FORMERLY HOME TO A BACHELOR, this Bel Air, California, residence included all the luxuries and amenities a single male could want, with the exception of the master suite. The original bath, with its poor design and much wasted space, was in desperate need of a makeover. To create separate his and her bathrooms and wardrobes, the homeowner called on Peter Sjöström of Peter Sjöström, AIA, Architecture & Design.

Sjöström reconfigured the original floor plan by incorporating a seldom-used gym adjacent to the master suite. The addition of this square footage allowed the architect to fashion separate his and her spaces. Within her bathroom (right), Sjöström incorporated large, single-piece slabs of statuary marble to the floors, wainscoting, and shower. The marble gives the room a feminine look, while Venetian plaster on the walls and ceiling furthers the rich ambiance of the space. Custom cabinetry and top-of-the-line Kohler fixtures imbue the room with a sense of luxury. In his bathroom, Azul Bahia granite evokes a masculine impression, and a steam shower (above) provides him with a private place to unwind. *Learn more about this designer at www.petersjostrom.com.* «

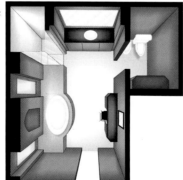

DESIGNER
Peter Sjöström AIA
Peter Sjöström AIA
Architecture & Design
1627 N. Gardner St.
Los Angeles, CA 90046

SPECIAL FEATURES
Single-piece slabs of statuary marble and Azul Bahia granite; Venetian plaster on walls and ceiling; custom cabinetry; Kohler fixtures

DIMENSIONS
17'6" x 17'6"

PRODUCTS USED
Cabinetry: Custom
Flooring: Statuary marble, Azul Bahia granite
Vanity Tops: Statuary marble
Sinks: Kohler
Plumbing Fixtures: Kohler
Tub: Americh
Shower Door: Custom
Toilet: Kohler
Mirrors: Custom beveled
Wallcovering: Venetian plaster
Backsplash/Tile: Statuary marble, Azul Bahia granite

Rocky Mountain Retreat

SITUATED AMID THE PICTURESQUE LANDSCAPE of the Rocky Mountains, this vacation house is owned by active homeowners who relish the many outdoor activities the area has to offer. From skiing to hiking, they enjoy it all. And following their outdoor adventures, they want to retreat to the master bathroom for a soothing soak or invigorating shower. So to create an indulgent yet fully functional space, the homeowners called on Linda Miller of Aspen Grove Kitchen & Bath, Inc.

Although the original bathroom boasted space and luxury, the small his and her vanities did not maximize storage potential. So to provide additional storage while maintaining an opulent, decorative aesthetic, Miller designed pullout columns with adjustable shelves for each side of the mirror. This configuration allows for easy access to cosmetics and other bath products. She then bridged the columns with a matching wood valance, creating the appearance of a custom, built-in furniture piece. Onyx lavs and countertops complement the onyx tile throughout and further the look of luxe. The result is a fully functional master bathroom that meets the needs of the homeowners while exuding a spalike atmosphere that one might expect from an upscale mountain retreat. *Learn more about this designer at www.aspengrovekitchenandbath.com.* «

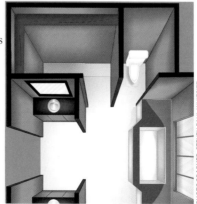

DESIGNER
Linda G. Miller,
ASID Allied Member
Aspen Grove Kitchen
& Bath, Inc.
721 Granite St., #A
Frisco, CO 80443
970.468.5393

SPECIAL FEATURES
Onyx tile countertops
and vessel sinks;
cherry wood cabinets;
pullout shelving behind
decorative columns on
each side of the mirror

DIMENSIONS
12' x 22'

PRODUCTS USED
Cabinetry: Medallion
Designer, Sonoma
Cherry, Pecan finish
Flooring: Travertine,
green onyx
Vanity Tops: Green onyx
Plumbing Fixtures:
Kohler
Tub: Kohler
Hardware: Emtek
Backsplash/Tile: Onyx
Plumbing Supplies:
Kohler

MEMBER OF
SEN DESIGN GROUP

PHOTOGRAPHER: STEVEN PAUL WHITSITT

Glassy Getaway

DESIGNERS
Heather McKinney, FAIA, LEED AP
Will Wood, AIA
McKinney York Architects
1301 E. Seventh St.
Austin, TX 78702
512.476.0201

M. Robbins Black, ASID, IIDA, RID
M. Robbins Black Interior Design
102 Downing Dr.
San Antonio, TX 78209
210.826.2100

Buddy Kinder
Signature Homes by Buddy Kinder
226 Farne Castle
Shavano Park, TX 78249
210.930.2777

SPECIAL FEATURES
A modern structure suitable for displaying the client's art-glass collection; custom cabinetry

DIMENSIONS
12'9" x 20'

PRODUCTS USED
Cabinetry: QSI Custom Cabinets
Flooring: Santenay French Limestone
Wall: Interstyle Watercolors glass tile in Dove
Vanity Tops: Silestone
Sinks: Kohler
Tub: Jado Glance Roman tub
Toilet: Toto Drake
Lighting: Flos
Hardware: Omnia

An avid collector of art glass, this Texas client is passionate about the many gorgeous pieces she has picked up over the years. Emphasized by sensual lines and striking colors, her artful assemblage can be found throughout the house. So when it came time to design her master bath, she wanted to extend those same sinuous lines into that room. To ensure her style was reflected in the best possible light, the owner called upon Heather McKinney, FAIA, LEED AP, and Will Wood, AIA, of McKinney York Architects for the project.

Mindful of their client's wish to incorporate her signature look, the design team translated her vision with scrupulous care. By melding French limestone with glass tiles, they created a soothing material palette. Custom-crafted cabinets "float" above the floor, further underscoring the room's graceful demeanor. Besides looking lovely, they also take care of the homeowner's storage needs. A small TV hides behind a mirror. Opposite the bath, an exercise area overlooks the pool, and the windows allow rays of light to dance nimbly amid this tastefully adorned space, looking every bit like the oasis that everyone imagined. *Learn more about McKinney York Architects at www.mckinneyyork.com.* «

PHOTOGRAPHER: THOMAS McCONNELL PHOTOGRAPHY

DESIGNER
Peter Ross Salerno,
CMKBD
Peter Salerno, Inc.
511 Goffle Rd.
Wyckoff, NJ 07481
201.251.6608

Shannon Gallagher Hall
Shannon Hall Designs
179 Scott St.
Daniel Island
Charleston, SC 29492

SPECIAL FEATURES
Oak island; his and her
vanities; chandelier and
other custom lighting

DIMENSIONS
18' x 19'

PRODUCTS USED
Cabinetry: Kraft-Maid
Cabinetry in maplewood
painted white for
vanities and quarter-
sawn white oak for the
island
Flooring: Limestone with
insert tiles, stones, and
pewter accents
Vanity Tops: Imperial
Green marble
Sinks: Kohler
Plumbing Fixtures: Perrin
& Rowe
Tub: Waterworks Empire
freestanding rectangular
bathtub
Shower Door: Perrin &
Rowe
Toilet: Toto
Lighting: Custom
Mirrors: Kraft-Maid
Cabinetry
Windows: Oslo

The 'Suite' Life

THIS COUPLE and their large, busy family needed a luxurious space to escape and relax. Their master bath, built by Roger Polo of Polo Master Builders, has luxury and space to spare. In fact, the biggest challenge these homeowners faced was deciding what to do with so much of it.

Designer Peter Ross Salerno, CMKBD, found the solution with a large freestanding island. Its quartersawn white oak matches the double doors leading into the bath, lending a sense of continuity with the bedroom. On either side of the island are two large maple vanities painted white. Each has Imperial Green marble tops, double medicine cabinets, and massive framed mirrors, providing each spouse his and her own space.

The room is fitted with custom lighting throughout, including a chandelier above the island. The large windows and light limestone tiles, stones, and pewter accents contribute to the natural, soothing tone. The tub niche next to the windows is set off by custom half-walls and columns on each side of the freestanding Empire tub. The shower and toilet are both set at diagonals in opposite corners to soften the shape of the room and preserve comfortable walking room in this sleek, calming retreat. *Learn more about this designer at www.petersalernoinc.com.* «

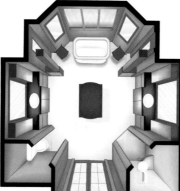

Bathed in Light

WHEN THIS ILLINOIS HOMEOWNER decided to update her master bath suite, she desired a design that could transform as her needs changed. So she hired designer Gary Lichlyter of Lemont Kitchen & Bath, who helped her create a refined space capable of serving into the future.

The remodel required the creation of additional storage space and wheelchair accessibility. To open up the bathroom, Lichlyter moved every plumbing location. His and her sinks share a single wall with beveled-glass mirrored medicine cabinets recessed into the wainscoting. A custom armoire provides extra storage. An LCD television is tucked into a shallow cabinet at the end of the tub. These alterations allow for a large door-free shower. Multiple hand-held body sprayers create a truly spalike experience.

Other accents include furniture-grade cabinetry, which connects the room with the rest of the home. Panels near the tub and toilet have full-length mirrors for easy wardrobe checks. The limestone floor-warming system keeps feet cozy year-round, and a towel radiator warms both towels and the room. With such efficient use of space, deluxe and adaptable amenities, and timeless style, this homeowner received the update of her dreams. *Learn more about this designer at www.lemontkitchenandbath.com.* «

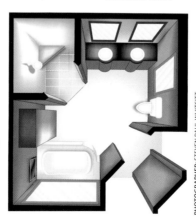

DESIGNER
Gary A. Lichlyter
Lemont Kitchen & Bath
106 Stephen St.
Lemont, IL 60439
630.257.8144

SPECIAL FEATURES
Radiant-heated limestone floors; spalike open shower; mirrored walls; inset television

DIMENSIONS
24' x 17'

PRODUCTS USED
Cabinetry: Jay Rambo Cabinet Co.
Flooring: Limestone
Vanity Tops: Quartz
Sinks: American Standard Ovalyn
Plumbing Fixtures: Rohl Country Bath Collection
Medicine Cabinets: Robern with beveled glass mirror
Tub: MTI Solitude soaker tub
Toilet: Toto Lloyd universal height
Towel Warmer: Zehnder
Floor Warming: Warmly Yours
Other: Jaclo grab bars

MEMBER OF
SEN DESIGN GROUP

PHOTOGRAPHER: STEVEN PAUL WHITSITT

PHOTOGRAPHER: STEVEN PAUL WHITSITT

Classic Luxury

THESE HOMEOWNERS TRAVEL overseas often, staying at some of the finer hotels in Europe. When the bathroom in their Illinois home began to feel dated, they challenged designer Tom Kindred of Kindred Kitchens and Baths to create Old World style with elegant amenities akin to those found in their favorite hotels. What they got was an entirely new sanctuary that met both of their needs.

To start, the vanities became separate for a his and her arrangement. Two walk-in closets were redesigned with masculine and feminine touches to meet differing needs. The wife enjoys the Bubble Massage tub for full relaxation, and the husband prefers the custom steam shower with multiple showerheads—both fixtures are in view of a fireplace and television. The space is kept cozy with warmed floors and rich cherry espresso cabinets, while chrome fixtures dazzle against the clean white Carrara marble.

The bathroom's new chic amenities are highlighted by natural light from a window that offers a view of private woods outside. The entryway between the rooms was transformed into an arched French door.

Now when these homeowners return home from their travels, they no longer have to leave the luxury behind. *Learn more about these designers at www.kindredkitchens.com.* «

DESIGNER
Tom Kindred
Kindred Kitchens and Baths
17625 Rt. 84 North
East Moline, IL 61244
309.737.1423

SPECIAL FEATURES
His and her vanities; steam shower with rain head; fireplace; heated floors; bubble massage tub; arched barreled ceilings; walk-in closets; crystal chandeliers; coffee bar

DIMENSIONS
23' x 18'

PRODUCTS USED
Cabinetry: Medallion Designer Gold in Espresso
Flooring: 18" x 18" Carrera marble with black granite accents
Vanity Tops: Carrera marble with ogee detail
Sinks: Kohler Memoirs
Plumbing Fixtures: Newport Brass in chrome
Tub: Kohler Memoirs Bubble Massage
Shower Door: European Custom frameless
Toilet: Kohler Memoirs
Lighting: Restoration Hardware
Hardware: Atlas Homewares chrome mega pulls
Mirrors: Custom
Backsplash/Tile: Carrera marble with chair and pencil accents
Plumbing Supplies: Newport Brass in chrome
Steam Shower: Kohler
Towel Warmer and Floor Heat: Warmly Yours
Closets: Closets Plus
Vents: Fantech
Fireplace: Regency
Windows: Pella

MEMBER OF
SEN DESIGN GROUP

Relaxation Ever After

To transform this spacious bathroom into a soothing retreat, the homeowners wanted to customize every detail from functionality to color. Designer Waine P. Hicks of W. P. Hicks Construction, Inc., helped realize their vision with a total remodel that focused on elegant detail and total relaxation.

Refreshing the cabinetry was simple in comparison to the complete restructuring of the shower, tub, and vanities with luxurious accents. The vented gas fireplace called for Hicks to rework the framing of the wall to accommodate a roof exhaust flue. In addition, he built a nook for the TV. Both appliances are remote controlled and elevated 30 inches for maximum view from the tub. On either side of the tub are his and her vanities in Picasso Cream marble with custom sink detailing to create depth. Behind the tub is a large shower with two entrances at either end, two showerheads, and custom polished-travertine shelves accented by polished-travertine floors throughout the bathroom.

All of the features center on the hand-laid mosaic tiling in the shower, which, when seen from the bedroom, is framed by a glass partition above the bath. This detail demanded exquisite craftsmanship and careful attention to preexisting concrete floors, and it ultimately became the focal point of this one-of-a-kind oasis. *Learn more about this designer at www.wphicks. com.* «

DESIGNER
Waine P. Hicks
W. P. Hicks Construction, Inc.
5686 Fruitville Rd.
Sarasota, FL 34232
941.378.3258

SPECIAL FEATURES
Remote-controlled natural gas fireplace; custom inset entertainment center; unique mosaic-tile design in the shower

DIMENSIONS
14' x 16'

PRODUCTS USED
Flooring: Travertine marble
Vanity Tops: Picasso Cream marble
Sinks: Toto
Plumbing Fixtures: Rohl

MEMBER OF
SEN DESIGN GROUP

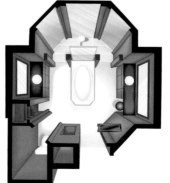

PHOTOGRAPHER: CHUCK DENNER, SHINE MEDIA PRODUCTIONS

Chic Antique

FOR THEIR MASTER SUITE PROJECT, these Pennsylvania homeowners asked David Stimmel of Stimmel Consulting Group to design a truly one-of-a-kind chateau-inspired retreat. While creating that exclusive look is difficult, Stimmel's real challenge was to echo a theme seen throughout the rest of the home: architectural antiques installed by the original builder. The different styles used around the house allowed for flexibility in mixing modern and antique themes.

Consistent minimalism refocused the space to the interesting architecture, which was obscured by the original design. The existing bath was gutted, along with a bedroom and a third-floor chamber above to create one large area while exposing a portion of the chimney. Wood beams salvaged from a circa-1850 barn add interest to the ceiling. The new bathroom and bedroom spaces are separated by a gas fireplace set off by Palladian glass in a brick pattern to mimic the chimney. The brick theme continues with a custom blend of tiles that forms an unusual vanity at the rear of the bath island.

Other patterns repeat to unify the space in surprising ways. The oval shower picks up on the round turrets visible through the windows and skylight. These subtle patterns and sleek design create a modern escape for this unique home. *Learn more about this designer at www.stimmeldesign.com.* «

DESIGNER
David Stimmel
Stimmel Consulting
Group, Inc.
855 Lewis Ln.
Ambler, PA 19002
215.542.0772

1042 Lancaster Ave.
Bryn Mawr, PA 19004
267.718.0479

SPECIAL FEATURES
Minimalist design; wood beams salvaged from a circa-1850 barn; custom tile blend

DIMENSIONS
10' x 18'3"

PRODUCTS USED
Cabinetry: Crystal Cabinet Works, Inc.
Sinks: Kohler
Hardware: Siro
Fireplace: Heat & Glo
Tile: Oceanside glass; Keshi Gold ceramic by Gravena
Marble: Custom-blend by Johanne Hudson
Granite: Absolute black by Marble Concepts
Faucets: Dornbracht

PHOTOGRAPHER: CHARLES MEACHAM

Total Restoration

DESIGNER
Barry Miller
Simply Baths &
Showcase Kitchens
630 Main St.
Monroe, CT 06468
203.445.2902

SPECIAL FEATURES
Frameless shower
and shower seat;
hydrotherapy heated
tub; make-up bench;
cathedral ceiling and
skylight

DIMENSIONS
13'2" x 11'4"

PRODUCTS USED
Cabinetry: Holiday Estate
Petersburg Square in
cherry with meadow
stain
Flooring: Lithos
porcelain tile with AKDO
border
Wall tile: Lithos sand
porcelain tile with AKDO
Emperador dark and
light bolish and dot-and-
dash listel
Vanity Tops: Brown onyx
Sinks: Dreamline
Emperador dark vessel
sinks
Plumbing Fixtures: Brizo
RSVP
Ventilation: Fantech
remote vent fan
Tub: Jason Int'l Designer
Collection
Shower Door: Frameless
**Shower Faucet and Tub
Filler:** Brizo RSVP
Shower Body Jets: Kohler
water tiles
Toilet: Toto Aquia II
Mirrors: Dreamline
Emperador dark marble
mirrors

MEMBER OF
SEN DESIGN GROUP

GROWING TIRED OF THEIR HOME'S GENERIC FINISHES, these Connecticut homeowners first worked with designer Barry Miller of Simply Baths & Showcase Kitchens on their kitchen remodel. During the project, they installed radiant heat in the master bathroom above it, which made remodeling the rest of the room more efficient and convenient. It also inspired the homeowners to give their bath personality.

Miller worked with the owners to make the space more upscale and contemporary, adding features as fashionable as they are functional. With the original square footage and a similar layout, Miller's new design altered the existing tub deck to accommodate a larger, frameless shower with a shower seat. For a sleek, spalike look, they used Kohler's jetted water tiles in the shower. The new hydrotherapy tub has a heater to keep the water warm. The master bathroom also features a brown onyx tub deck and countertops, marble vessel sinks, marble mirrors, and a makeup bench. The cathedral ceiling and skylight add a light, airy atmosphere to the room.

By making the most of the existing space, the homeowners have a relaxing retreat they love. *Learn more about this designer at www.simplybaths.net and www.myshowcasekitchen.com.* «

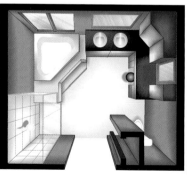

PHOTOGRAPHER: CHRIS WARE, CHRIS WARE PHOTOGRAPHY, LLC

Bathed in Light

As EMPTY NESTERS, these homeowners wanted to update their existing space to use it to its fullest potential while incorporating several specific wishes: more storage, furniture-style vanities, stonelike tile, and better lighting.

Storage was an integral first step to making the room functional. Cabinets for storage at the vanity area on either side of the sinks feature a canopy that contains task lighting. Casement windows and plantation shutters behind the tub allow natural light to flow into the room and highlight many fine details. Malibu granite countertops and a complementary backsplash add warmth and contrast to the space. Sconce lighting and matching decorative mirror frames complete the soothing style the clients desired.

The enlarged shower is tiled to the ceiling. Travertine accents combine with varied porcelain tile to create contrast and depth. Floor tile cut on a bias with round, bronze accents at every corner continue the eye-appealing visual effect.

The antique white cabinets, light-hued tiles, glass, and subtle lighting create a calming and relaxing atmosphere that redefines elegance. Classic details combine with modern functionality in this master bath. *Learn more about this designer at www.kitchenandbathconcepts.com.* «

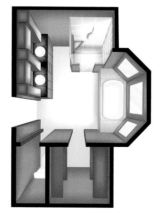

DESIGNER
Jim Meloy, CKD and
Courtney Foster
Kitchen and Bath
Concepts
11444 Alpharetta Hwy.
Roswell, GA 30076
770.442.9845

SPECIAL FEATURES
Vanity light canopy;
antique white cabinets;
casement windows

DIMENSIONS
8' x 13'

PRODUCTS USED
Cabinetry: Holiday
Kitchens
Flooring: NuTrav silver
tile
Vanity Tops: Malibu
granite
Sinks: Kohler
Plumbing Fixtures:
Santec Monarch Series
Tubs: MTI
Shower Door: Frameless
Toilet: Kohler
Lighting: Recessed cans,
sconces by owner
Faucets: Santec Monarch
Series

MEMBER OF
SEN DESIGN GROUP

PHOTOGRAPHER: JOHN UMBARGER

Multipurpose Room

FOR THIS COUPLE, entertaining guests almost every weekend is a real joy. To make their home as hospitable to their guests as possible, they hired German Brun and Lizmarie Esparza of Den Architecture to undertake a complete redesign of their kitchen and bathrooms. Needing a multipurpose powder room, they asked the design team to create a transitional bathroom accessible from the house and the pool area with a level of formality suitable for both. They also wanted the space to eventually serve as a bathroom for their young child.

Brun and Esparza used the homeowners pool as inspiration while choosing forms and finishes. A long white vanity cantilevers from the wall much like a diving board. The shower niche, also in white, welcomes guests returning from a day outdoors, and aqua glass mosaic tiles wash the main wall with color. From a sustainability standpoint, stock cabinets and shelves are flexible and reusable. Caribbean coral stone, a refined version of the pool deck material, was used for the flooring. And the overall pale palette's high reflectivity allows for daylight to save energy.

The end result combines the couple's requests in a playful balance of formal compositions and casual materials. *Learn more about this designer at www.den-arc.com.* «

DESIGNER
German Brun
Lizmarie Esparza
Den Architecture
350 S. Miami Ave.
Miami, FL 33130
305.335.6085

SPECIAL FEATURES
Bathroom with dual accessibility to home and outdoor pool area; pool-inspired color palette; off-the-shelf vanity made unique with custom-built shadow boxes; eco-friendly features

DIMENSIONS
6' x 8'

PRODUCTS USED
Plumbing Fixtures: Kohler
Tub: Kohler
Shower Door: Custom frameless enclosure
Toilet: Toto
Hardware: Solid aluminum pulls by Cook Knobs
Mirrors: Tightlines Wood Works, custom

PHOTOGRAPHER: GREG CLARK PHOTOGRAPHY

Historic Renovation

REMODELER

Charlie Allen
Charlie Allen
Restorations
91 River St.
Cambridge, MA 02139
617.661.7411

SPECIAL FEATURES

Countertop and apron crafted from a single piece of Azul Cielo marble; luxurious soaking tub; elegant Ann Sacks wall tile

DIMENSIONS

9' x 12'

PRODUCTS USED

Cabinetry: Robern medicine cabinet
Flooring: Ann Sacks mosaic mini brick tile in White Thassos
Vanity Tops: Azul Cielo marble
Sinks: Kohler Caxton
Faucets: Dornbracht Tara
Tub: Burgbad Solitaire Selection Crono 2.0 in Alpine White
Shower Door: Prestige Custom Glass and Mirror
Plumbing Fixtures: Hans Grohe showerhead, Clubmaster shower control, Dornbracht Tara pressure-balance shower valve in chrome
Toilet: Toto Aquia
Towel Warmer: Myson Avonmore contemporary electric towel warmer with smart thermo control
Backsplash: Ann Sacks Metro Crisp in Skim Milk Glossy

THIS SMALL FAMILY loved the rich history of their 95-year-old house, but they weren't as fond of the bathroom's dated design. Seeking a simple and bright spa-inspired space, they hired Charlie Allen of Charlie Allen Restorations to complete an overhaul of historic proportions, which started with a full gut of the room and reframing of the entire floor. To achieve the clean look, the room's lines had to be perfectly level—a challenge in such an old house.

An elevator is located directly behind this second-floor bath, so the electrical and plumbing systems were run inside the shaft. Next, because it wouldn't fit through the doorway, the oversized soaker tub was brought in during the early phases of construction but wasn't installed until other work was completed. Its placement is beneath a window, so the glass panes were swapped for safer tempered glass.

Also on Allen's task list was to supply a surplus of storage without cluttering the room with too much cabinetry. His solution: a vanity base, medicine cabinets in the wraparound mirror, and a closed cabinet at the bottom of a shelf tower. Finally, a meticulous mix of ambient, task, and natural lighting helps put a fresh new look on this old home's master bath. *Learn more about this remodeler at www.charlie-allen.com.* «

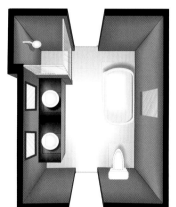

PHOTOGRAPHER: SHELLY HARRISON PHOTOGRAPHY

International Inspiration

WHEN ENVISIONING A NEW STYLE for their master suite, this couple from Patagonia wanted to balance the charming ruggedness of South America with the sophistication of urban life in the United States. Hiring German Brun and Lizmarie Esparza of Den Architecture, they tasked the designers with completing the remodel on their tight budget. So they decided to keep existing plumbing to reduce labor costs, repurpose the large existing mirror, and incorporate prefabricated components from local retailers.

With their game plan in place, product selection began. As a starting point, the clients selected a mosaic slate that reflected the rock formations and color spectrum of the Andes Mountains. The slate's horizontal striations and layering of colors provided the inspiration for the rest of the suite's style. A series of horizontal elements combining solids and voids include mirrors, cabinets, and shelves. Tones of acorn brown and off white exude rustic appeal while chrome accents in the fixtures, accessories, and lighting add a touch of refinement. Finally, the same flooring was extended to the glass-enclosed shower to increase the perception of space.

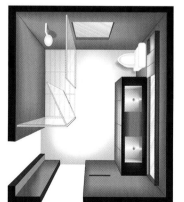

With their internationally inspired suite complete, this couple enjoys the best of both worlds every time they step into their bathroom. *Learn more about this designer at www.den-arc.com.* «

DESIGNER
German Brun
Lizmarie Esparza
Den Architecture
350 S. Miami Ave.
Miami, FL 33130
305.335.6085

SPECIAL FEATURES
Style inspiration from South America; off-the-shelf components customized for the space; design utilizes daylighting to reduce electricity consumption

DIMENSIONS
11' x 11'

PRODUCTS USED
Plumbing Fixtures: Kohler
Tub: Kohler
Shower Door: Custom frameless enclosure
Toilet: Toto
Hardware: Solid aluminum pulls by Cook Knobs
Mirrors: Tightlines Wood Works custom

Down to the Details

FOR THIS PROFESSIONAL COUPLE, having a private oasis where they could wash away the workweek was their top priority. But their current bathroom wasn't cutting it. So as they undertook a whole house remodel, which included a full gut, new wiring, and new plumbing, they paid particular attention to the details of their master bath. To help them tie it all together, they worked with designer Dan Diewald of Best Cabinets.

They hired Best Cabinets because one of their main design desires was for custom-finished, high-quality cabinetry with exact specifications on drawer and door hardware. Diewald fulfilled the homeowners' requests by painting a one-of-a-kind white finish over the maple cabinets and outfitting them in Blum hardware that features full extension with an undermount soft-close feature.

Another of the homeowners' design requests for the cabinetry was a staggered look, which was challenging due to minimal space. Diewald was able to incorporate the full overlay fronts, but the stepped drawers were a close fit. Finishing off their vision for the overall aesthetic, the clients designed a herringbone pattern in the new marble floor.

Combining their details with Diewald's professional installations, this couple's creative vision is now complete. *Learn more about this designer at www.thebestcabinets.com.* «

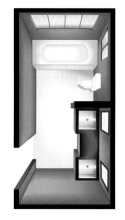

DESIGNER
Dan Diewald
Best Cabinets
1500 W. Cortland St.
Chicago, IL 60642
877.808.8818

SPECIAL FEATURES
Custom cabinetry finish; stepped look in minimal space; herringbone pattern in marble flooring

DIMENSIONS
5' x 8'

PRODUCTS USED
Cabinetry: Best Cabinets
Flooring: Marble with herringbone pattern
Vanity Tops: Marble
Sinks: Undermount
Faucets: Chrome
Hardware: Best Cabinets

PHOTOGRAPHER: JOE NOEL

Soothing Suite

WITH THEIR TWO CHILDREN GROWN and moved out of the house, these empty nesters decided to feather their nest all for themselves. With their house quieter and calmer than it had been during their busy child-rearing years, they decided to supplement the serenity by transforming their master bathroom into a spa suite built especially for the two of them. To create their tranquil retreat, they worked with designer Abbey Weiss of Bella Domicile, Inc., who faced this challenge: she couldn't relocate the plumbing fixtures. She also needed to add adequate, accessible storage to keep the environment clear of clutter.

To open and unify the area, she removed one wall entirely. To further the feel of unity for the design and for the couple, she incorporated a custom trough-style sink with two faucets, which allow them to use the sink at the same time. The toilet, which couldn't be moved, blocked the lower portion of the tall storage cabinet. As a solution, Weiss replaced it with a smaller toilet and added special-size doors on the base cabinets for easy access. To deliver the storage surplus requested, she also added a pullout vanity grooming cabinet that houses a curling iron, blow dryer, and other makeup items.

With their bathroom remodeled for pampering, this couple is relaxing now more than ever before. *Learn more about this designer at www.belladomicile.com.* «

DESIGNER
Abbey Weiss
Bella Domicile, Inc.
6210 Nesbitt Rd.
Madison, WI 53719
608.271.8241

SPECIAL FEATURES
Custom Corian trough-style sink; grooming cabinet; small-size toilet

DIMENSIONS
7' x 8'

PRODUCTS USED
Cabinetry: Dura Supreme Crestwood in cherry wood
Flooring: Roma SAL Caffe tile
Vanity Tops: Corian in Tumbleweed
Sinks: Corian in Tumbleweed
Faucets: Kohler Forte in brushed nickel
Shower Door: Hellenbrand Glass, LLC, custom enclosure
Shower Walls: Roma SAL Caffe tile and Roma TUM Pebble in Baja Cream
Toilet: Kohler Persuade
Lighting: Kovacs Bath Fixtures vertical mounted
Mirrors: Dura Supreme frames
Wallcovering: Roma SAL Caffe tile

MEMBER OF
SEN DESIGN GROUP

PHOTOGRAPHER: MARCIA HANSEN, MARCIA HANSEN PHOTOGRAPHIC CO, LLC

Balinese Bath

DESIGNER
Laura Brooks Meyer, IIDA
Molly Richter, Project
Manager
Meyer & Meyer, Inc.,
Architecture & Interiors
396 Commonwealth Ave.
Boston, MA 02215
617.266.0555

SPECIAL FEATURES
Balinese style, exotic
sapele wood; textured
river stone on shower
floor; intricate
fireplace; yoga studio;
homeowners' private art
collection worked into
design

DIMENSIONS
20' x 30'

PRODUCTS USED
Cabinetry: Sapele wood
Flooring: Sapele wood
Vanity Tops: Black
Vermont slate
Shower Floor: Textured
river stone
Shower Walls: Black
Vermont slate
Fireplace: Rough-hewn
granite
Wallcovering: Sapele
wood
Blinds: Scented natural
fiber

WORLD TRAVELERS AND AVID ART COLLECTORS, these
homeowners were inspired by a trip to remodel their master
bath and bedroom in the spirit and style of Bali architecture
and design. To create their exotic escape, they hired Laura
Brooks Meyer, IIDA, and Molly Richter of Meyer &
Meyer, Inc., Architecture & Interiors, a firm known for its
artistic and innovative solutions.

In the bath, the design team covered the walls, floors,
and vanity in sapele wood. For rich contrast, the countertops
and shower walls are finished in black Vermont slate. The
shower floor of textured river stones massages the feet,
letting stress seep away. A fireplace of rough-hewn granite
with an inlaid carved-limestone relic depicting an ancient
ceremony adds warmth and flickering light for atmosphere,
which is enhanced by scented natural-fiber blinds that filter
natural light and add a spiritual ambiance. The suite has a
yoga studio surrounded by built-in benches
adorned with richly embroidered Balinese
pillows. An antique door, heavily carved
with Indonesian designs, is mounted to a
cabinet door housing yoga mats.

These elements, along with
incorporated artifacts from the clients'
travels, bring the true beauty of Bali into
this new bath. *Learn more about this designer
at www.meyerandmeyerarchitects.com.* «

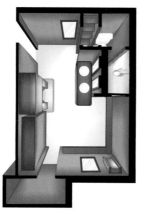

PHOTOGRAPHER: LAURA MOSS

Star Gazer

THIS BEAUTIFUL MASTER BATH in a Farmington, Connecticut, grand colonial was anything but grand. Much to the chagrin of the young, professional homeowners, the former '80s-style room boasted a large burgundy whirlpool tub and flimsy plastic shower. To transform the space, the homeowners called on Lorey Cavanaugh and the design team of Kitchen and Bath Design Consultants LLC. The couples' stated goals: create an elegant retreat with generous views to the wooded backyard, provide separate vanity spaces, each with ample storage, and include a separate tub and shower.

Cavanaugh and her team achieved these goals by installing a three-panel casement window to flood the room with natural light, maximize the view to the backyard, and allow for stargazing from the tub. The shower and tub share a serpentine deck, which creates a seat in the shower and a comfy transition wedge into the tub. The tile work on the tub surround and in the shower adds an array of elegant, custom details. A generous furniture-style double vanity provides abundant storage and ample countertop space. Additional details, including turned legs, contribute to the graceful ambiance. In the end, the clients were thrilled with the result, which delivered all of their stated objectives and then some. «

DESIGNER
Lorey Cavanaugh, CKD/CBD
Kitchen and Bath Design Consultants LLC
1000 Farmington Ave.
West Hartford, CT 06107
860.232.2872

SPECIAL FEATURES
Curved whirlpool tub surrounded with intricately tiled skirt; custom shower with exquisite tile detail; generously scaled, cantilevered vanity area

DIMENSIONS
10' x 12'

PRODUCTS USED
Tile: Tumbled almond beige, Malaga Cove in sage pearl beach glass, Rifles Perla shower tile
Cabinetry: Ultracraft, Dayton Door, maple in Sand Brown Glaze
Mirrors: Robern
Sinks: Kohler Devonshire
Tub: BainUltra
Toilet: Kohler Serif
Shower Door: Custom
Vanity Tops, Tub Deck: LG Hi Macs in Moonscape
Lights: Forecast
Plumbing Supplies: Kohler
Drawer Pulls: Richelieu
Knobs: Richelieu
Towel Radiator: Zehnder
Showerpan: Maluku
Window: Vetter Casements
Flooring: Daltile Continental slate, Egyptian beige
In-floor heating: Warmly Yours

MEMBER OF
SEN DESIGN GROUP

PHOTOGRAPHER: OLSON PHOTOGRAPHIC LLC

Natural & Dynamic

When this single mom of boys decided to remodel her bathroom, she commissioned Ricki Weber of Baths by RJ to create her at-home haven. This room was the predictable builder's version of a "luxury" master bath. It had all five fixtures shoe-horned into a too-small 9×11-foot layout, leaving it without any space to move around, much less enjoy. The style was also typical of a standard builder's bathroom—it was neutral and bland. The shower had the feel of a small, dark closet.

Expanding was not a possibility, so this client made a bold decision. The homeowner decided space, comfort and usability were far more important than the number of fixtures. The solution: eliminate the second sink and tub. The result: a large shower with a bench, as well as a comfortable place to sit at the vanity, both very well lit. The room now boasts a sense of spaciousness. The colors and textures bring vibrance to the room, while the natural materials add a look of timelessness. This satisfied client now starts each day in a bathroom she thoroughly enjoys, and one that specifically reflects her natural and dynamic attitude toward life. «

DESIGNER
Ricki Weber
Baths by RJ
3975 University Dr.
Fairfax, VA 22030
703.352.8680

SPECIAL FEATURES
Two-level vanity; bench in shower

DIMENSIONS
9' x 11'

PRODUCTS USED
Tile: Rex Ceramica, porcelain, glass tile detail in wall
Cabinetry: Kraftmaid
Sink: Kohler
Faucets: Kohler
Toilet: Kohler
Shower Door: Century
Vanity Tops: Granite
Flooring: Rex Ceramica, porcelain
Plumbing Supplies: Kohler

MEMBER OF
SEN DESIGN GROUP

Nautical Niche

THE OWNERS OF THIS CAPE COD HOUSE selected Mariette Barsoum of Divine Kitchens LLC to create a master bathroom where they could retreat after a day in the sun. They also wanted it to reflect the seascape that surrounded them. The cabinets feature custom recessed-panel painted doors in full overlay construction. The spacious vanity offers ample storage in banks of drawers and double-door cabinets. Open shelving and glass-fronted counter cabinets provide additional storage and display space.

The large walk-in shower is encased by soft-hued ceramic tile and glass and features a fabulous rainfall showerhead. The marvelous front facade of the tub shares the same cabinetry panels as the vanity. The tub is decked with more of the same marble and completed by a ceramic tile backsplash. The large shower and whirlpool tub are truly luxurious. Open shelves at the end of the tub provide extra storage for towels, bath oils, and candles. Crisp white-painted cabinetry, oil-rubbed bronze fixtures, and whimsical nautical accents create a peaceful yet stylish master bath that is very much at home in this beachside abode. «

DESIGNER
Mariette Barsoum
Divine Kitchens LLC
40 Lyman St.
Westborough, MA 01581
508.366.5670

SPECIAL FEATURES
Custom double sink vanity with open shelving for display and glass-front cabinets for additional storage; large glass shower with rainfall showerhead

DIMENSIONS
8' x 16'6"

PRODUCTS USED
Tile: Ceramic
Cabinetry: Custom
Vanity tops: Marble
Plumbing supplies: Oil-rubbed bronze, Grohe
Drawer pulls: Top Knobs

MEMBER OF
SEN DESIGN GROUP

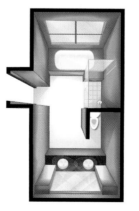

PHOTOGRAPHER: LORETTA BERARDINELLI

Revamped Retreat

FOR THIS LANGHORNE, PENNSYLVANIA, couple, a complete overhaul and upgrade of their master bath was at the top of their wish list. To make their revamped retreat a reality, they hired Wheeler Brothers Kitchen & Bath Design Center.

Gutting the space to start fresh, the designers faced a few challenges along the way, such as the removal of existing tile and underlayment that had been glued down to the subfloor. Interior changes prompted the moving and enlarging of a window to appear more aesthetically symmetrical in the room. Outside construction with siding and trim also had to be addressed. They also helped the owners work through a few compromises to accommodate the couple's wants and needs.

With solutions carried out for each of those issues, the rebuilding began. Coordinating tile, paint, and granite colors accomplished a relaxing but more modern look to complement the rest of the home's style. Semicustom cherry cabinetry with varying elevations and depths adds dimension, and custom built-in shelves with mirrors add an eye-pleasing flow from the tub surround into the shower area. A Schlueter waterproofing shower system and heated floors by Warmly Yours are other special touches that made this bath remodel a spa-inspired success.

Learn more about this designer at www.wheelerbci.com. «

DESIGNER
Wheeler Brothers Kitchen & Bath Design Center
151 Bellevue Ave.
Penndel, PA 19047
215.757.2144

SPECIAL FEATURES
Semicustom cherry cabinetry; custom built-in shelves with mirrors; Schlueter waterproofing shower system; heated floors by Warmly Yours

DIMENSIONS
13'9" x 11'9"

PRODUCTS USED
Cabinetry: Kabinart Arts and Crafts Cherry cabinets in Cinnamon
Flooring and Shower Walls: Tibet Beige Edilgres porcelein tile with mosaic accents from Tile Gallery
Vanity Tops: Typhoon Bordeaux granite from Stone Tec
Sinks: Kohler Ladena
Plumbing Fixtures: Delta Addison Collection
Tub: American Standard Reminiscence Oval
Tub Deck: Typhoon Bordeaux granite from Stone Tec
Custom Tub Panel: JH Construction & Millwork
Shower Door: Weise Glassworks LLC frameless
Shower Seat: Typhoon Bordeaux granite from Stone Tec
Toilet: Kohler Cimmaron
Lighting: Halo 4-inch recessed lights
Hardware: Tops Knobs, Delta
Mirrors: Weise Glassworks LLC
Wallcovering: Sherwin-Williams

MEMBER OF
SEN DESIGN GROUP

Restful Retreat

THIS REMODELING PROJECT began when a professional Tennessee couple decided to create a more open, inviting master bath for their home. Although their existing bathroom was large, it featured a dark, cavelike shower room and had small inefficient vanities. To design and construct their dream bath, the couple turned to Reed Thomas of Thomas Kitchen and Bath Inc. in Lebanon, Tennessee.

Thomas began by repositioning the shower to a spot where a large closet once stood. This new location provides the clients with an abundantly spacious design and thus successfully accomplishes their primary goal for the new layout. For a more functional living space, "his" vanity sits between ample windows while a new angled wall provides the space for "her" practical, easily accessible vanity space. The bath, a deep Hydro-Thermo massaging air tub by BainUltra, provides the perfect accessory for relaxation, which is a highly coveted element in the lives of this busy couple. Tying the room together are glaze-painted cabinetry, Cambria quartz countertops, Toto toilets, and large-tile flooring. The result is an immaculate design and a blissful couple. «

DESIGNER
Reed Thomas AKBD
Thomas Kitchen and
Bath Inc.
1417 W. Main St.
Lebanon, TN 37087
615.449.6554.

SPECIAL FEATURES
Spacious shower area;
air tub; quartz tops; Toto
fixtures

DIMENSIONS
21' x 12'

PRODUCTS USED
Cabinetry: Bertch Legacy
Flooring: AO Tile, Amita
Countertops: Cambria,
Victoria
Sinks: Toto
Toilet: Toto
Faucets: Danze
Tub: BainUltra
Vent/light: Panasonic

MEMBER OF
SEN DESIGN GROUP

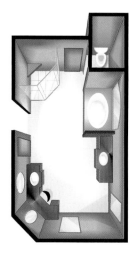

Detailed Delight

DETAILS ARE THE NAME OF THE GAME in this Lemont, Illinois bathroom designed by Jack Slubowski of Homewood Kitchen and Bath Inc. for his clients. To begin the project, Slubowski gutted the space, a necessity for the intricate remodel. Of the room's stunning features, the elaborate shower is one of the crown jewels. The homeowners, however, were concerned about the hot-water delivery. To alleviate their concerns, Slubowski installed a Noritz on-demand hot-water system. The next challenge was working within the tight space.

To make the most of the room, Slubowski incorporated a variety of unique details. An arched window situated next to the tub allows the clients to view the outdoors while bathing. For a timeless touch, the designer incorporated custom Shoji doors with rice-paper screens. A curved glass-block wall hides the water closet. And for added luxury, Slubowski installed a steam unit featuring water- and steam-proof speakers. Vaulted ceilings give the small space a large feel, and vanities with good task lighting top off the detailed bathroom. «

DESIGNER
Jack Slubowski
Homewood Kitchen and
Bath Inc.
18027 Dixie Hwy.
Homewood, IL 60430
708.799.0176

SPECIAL FEATURES
Arched window to view
outdoors from the tub;
custom Shoji doors
with rice paper screens;
floating vanities with
under-vanity lighting

DIMENSIONS
10' x 15'

PRODUCTS USED
Tile: Lippert granite
Cabinetry: The
Hampshire Company
Mirrors: The Hampshire
Company
Sinks: Kohler
Faucets: Grohe
Tub: Kohler
Toilets: Kohler
Shower door: Euroview
Vanity Tops: Rocka
granite
Flooring: Virginia
Lighting: Task
Glass Block: Block It

MEMBER OF
SEN DESIGN GROUP

PHOTOGRAPHER: STEVEN PAUL WHITSITT

Bright Light

WHEN THIS YOUNG FLORIDA COUPLE decided to improve their existing master bathroom, they hoped for a room designed to provide the elegance and privacy they deserved, as well as a fun area for their youngsters to enjoy. To make their dream a reality, the homeowners called on Walter Allan of Blossom Brothers Inc. Allan designed the couple's new luxurious master suite to include everything needed for a functional bathroom. He also incorporated an array of finishing touches to create the indulgent environment the clients desired.

Where a standard tub and detached shower once stood, Allan installed a luxurious whirlpool bath complemented by a spacious shower. The designer also incorporated a half wall, which separates the two areas and serves as a spray panel for the shower with a nook for shampoo and soap storage. A custom clear-glass panel keeps the look open. Allan split the cabinetry into wonderful his and her vanity arrangements, including a makeup area enhanced with natural light through the sliding doors leading to the pool. Finally, the water closet has a clipped corner entry for a wider main door and a full panoramic view from the bedroom entrance. The master bathroom is now a bright and spacious room the whole family can enjoy. «

DESIGNER
Walter Allan
Blossom Brothers Inc.
2706 N. Federal Hwy.
Delray Beach, FL 33483
561.274.7020

SPECIAL FEATURES
Private water closet; makeup area with natural light; decorative wall separating the tub and the shower

DIMENSIONS
12' x 16'

PRODUCTS USED
Cabinetry: UltraCraft
Sinks: Toto
Tub: Americh whirlpool
Toilet: Toto
Shower Door: Shower Doors Unlimited Inc.
Vanity Tops: LG Hi-Macs
Lights: Norwell
Plumbing: Brizo
Drawer Pulls: Top Knobs

MEMBER OF
SEN DESIGN GROUP

PHOTOGRAPHER: JIM GREENE

Beautiful Simplicity

WHEN THIS NEW JERSEY COUPLE decided to build a new house in Livingston, their builder recommended designer Amir Ilin of Küche+Cucina. After Ilin completed the kitchen design it was time to focus on the bathrooms. For this task, Ilin's wife, Anka, who is an interior designer, joined the team.

The clients' wish was to have a Zen-inspired or spalike retreat where they could start and end each day. With this in mind, the Ilins selected Pedini wood-colored textured laminate with aluminum handles and a dark Caesarstone vanity top. The vanity was positioned at the far end of the room to serve as a focal point and to allow for his and her sinks and to maximize storage space. To maintain an open, airy aesthetic, the Ilins mounted the cabinetry to the wall. Contrasting tiles break up the large room and satisfy the spa style: the darker tiles on the main section of the floor lend a ruglike feel, while the lighter tiles on the front of the tub lend light to the space. Other details, such as strategically placed stone pebbles, further the organic atmosphere, while high-tech amenities adapt the space for modern use.

With their bathroom transformed into their personal spa, this couple now has the relaxing master bath they desired. *Learn more about this designer at www.kuche-cucina.com.* «

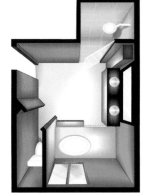

DESIGNER
Amir Ilin
Küche+Cucina
489 Rt. 17 South
Paramus, NJ 07652
201.261.5221

SPECIAL FEATURES
Glass mosaic wall; extra-large center island with concrete top; floating tilt shelves; white glass bifold wall cabinets

DIMENSIONS
13' x 18'

PRODUCTS USED
Cabinetry: Pedini Magika
Flooring: Porcelain
Vanity Tops: Caesarstone
Sinks: Kohler
Faucets: Kohler
Tub: Kohler
Shower Door: Custom
Toilet: Kohler
Hardware: Pedini Quadra
Mirrors: Custom

MEMBER OF
SEN DESIGN GROUP

PHOTOGRAPHER: KEN LAUBEN

Classic & Stately

To TRANSFORM THEIR BATHROOM into a luxurious retreat, the owners of this New Jersey home requested the help of Raymond Ferraro of All Trades Contracting. Ferraro began by completely gutting the room. He then placed the floor joists and demolished the walls. He also replaced the window with a smaller unit for privacy. By completely reconfiguring the fixture placement and plumbing, Ferraro was able to devise a highly functional layout.

In the shower, Ferraro incorporated an all-vinyl transom window. The window gives the clients a durable alternative for the bath area, where the combination of wood and water doesn't hold up well. Its awning style, high on the wall, opens out. Ferraro also increased the height of the built-in medicine cabinet, enlarging it from 30 to 40 inches. The 9-foot ceilings add to the grand feeling of the small room. A small soffit dropped into the shower allows just enough space for crown molding to top off this classic design. «

DESIGNER
Raymond Ferraro
All Trades Contracting
1335 Rt. 31 South
Annandale, NJ 08801
908.713.1584

SPECIAL FEATURES
Oversize shower;
transom window in
shower; open vanity
base; heated floor;
authentic crackle tile
with inset

DIMENSIONS
5' x 11'

PRODUCTS USED
Cabinetry: WoodPro
Mirrors: Affina
Sink: Kohler
Facuet: Elkay
Toilet: Kohler
Shower Door: Advanced
Glass
Vanity Tops: Marble
Flooring: Weaved marble
Plumbing Supplies: Moen

MEMBER OF
SEN DESIGN GROUP

California Contemporary

WHEN REMODELING THEIR 1960S HOME, these homeowners wanted to create a sleek, fresh look that complemented the residence's classic style while still fitting the needs of their family. The room that saw one of the most dramatic overhauls was the second-floor bathroom, which went from old-fashioned and inconvenient to a bona-fide masterpiece under the expertise of James Blakeley III, ASID, of Blakeley-Bazely, LTD.

In terms of home renovation, bathrooms can often pose some unique challenges, and this case was no different. Because Blakeley and his team couldn't move the plumbing lines, they worked with the existing layout to modernize the space. The first things to go were the outdated shower and tub. In their place, a new glass-walled standing shower and freestanding tub were installed, adding tranquility and sophistication to the space. The shower dam was removed, so the clean lines of the glass are never broken.

Other features that complete the streamlined, clean appearance are the custom Wenge wood cabinets topped with glass. The Wet Style sinks mirror the sleekness of the tub, which is also by Wet Style. To keep the look, the electrical receptacles are hidden in the vanity. The contemporary feel of the room is tied together with the paint and tile wallcovering and the Platinum Tile flooring. *Learn more about this designer at www.jamesblakeley.com.* «

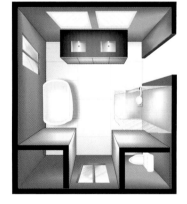

DESIGNER
James Blakeley III, ASID
Blakeley-Bazely, LTD
9663 Santa Monica Blvd.,
Ste. 687
Beverly Hills, CA 90210
323.653.3548

SPECIAL FEATURES
All-glass shower;
freestanding tub; vessel
sinks

DIMENSIONS
12' x 15'

PRODUCTS USED
Cabinetry: Custom
Wenge wood
Flooring: Platinum Tile
Vanity Top: Glass
Sink: Wet Style
Faucet: Gessi
Plumbing Supplies: Gessi
Tub: Wet Style
Shower Door: Custom
Toilet: Toto
Lighting: Halo
Hardware: Details
Mirrors: Rubon
Wallcovering: Paint, tile

PHOTOGRAPHER: MATTHEW KRANTZ

Sleek Organization

THESE CALIFORNIA HOMEOWNERS infused their home with the tranquility and style that matched their contemporary and minimal design; however, their master bathroom remained an eyesore. An open room with tons of space, it quickly became the home's catch-all for storage. Looking for a space-saving solution that would align with their aesthetic, they hired James Blakeley of Blakeley-Bazeley, LTD.

The largest obstacle that kept the space from serving the homeowners' needs was the lack of storage space. Towels and bathroom toiletries piled up, cluttering the countertops and making the room inefficient. To overcome this, Blakeley fully gutted and remodeled the space.

The new bathroom was outfitted with mirrored doors that keep the closet hidden. By tucking away the unsightly yet necessary features, the true gems of the bathroom remodel shine—the marble flooring, custom oak cabinetry, and marble counters. The Kohler tub, sinks, and toilet add continuity to the room, while the shower was custom designed. Halo lighting illuminates the space, adding to its depth and dimension. The result is an ingenious way to create more space and provide a clean, uncluttered look. *Learn more about this designer at www.jamesblakeley.com.* «

DESIGNER
James Blakeley III, ASID
Blakeley-Bazeley, LTD
9663 Santa Monica Blvd.,
Ste. 687
Beverly Hills, CA 90210
323.653.3548

SPECIAL FEATURES
Mirrored doors disguising the closet; hidden electrical receptacles located in vanity drawers; standing cabinets hold storage

DIMENSIONS
12' x 12'

PRODUCTS USED
Cabinetry: Custom Oak
Flooring: Marble
Vanity Tops: Marble
Sinks: Kohler
Faucets: Dornbracht
Plumbing Supplies: Dornbracht
Tub: Kohler
Shower Door: Custom
Toilet: Kohler
Lighting: Halo
Hardware: Details
Mirrors: Custom

Shining Design

THIS MASTER BATH started out as an incredibly outdated space, broken up into two small, difficult-to-navigate rooms. To make the space livable and beautiful, Barry Miller of Simply Baths redesigned the area for these Connecticut homeowners.

To create different zones within the bathroom, Miller removed some walls and placed the toilet in a private space with a window. A French door allows natural illumination to filter through to the rest of the bath, as does the skylight, which is strategically positioned above the tub.

Porcelain tile provides the distinguished look of tumbled marble at a lower cost and with less maintenance. The roomy shower with its built-in bench is the ideal place to unwind after a long day.

The rich cherry cabinetry is the perfect complement to the warm-toned porcelain tile, which leads right up to the luxuriously large soaking tub.

Even though the overall square footage remained the same after the remodel, the space is now better lit and feels much more spacious. And the homeowners couldn't be happier about their redone retreat. «

DESIGNER
Barry Miller
Simply Baths, a division
of The Brush's End Inc.
37A Padnaram Rd.
Danbury, CT 06811
203.792.2691

SPECIAL FEATURES
Spacious bath with an integrated platform tub and shower

DIMENSIONS
9' x 14'

PRODUCTS USED
Cabinetry: Woodpro, Nottingham, cherry sable finish
Flooring: Porcelain tile, Panaria-Amber Fiorita
Countertops and Tub Deck: Caesarstone Champagne limestone
Sinks: Kohler Caxton
Faucets: Danze Fairmont brushed nickel
Bathtub: MTI Victoria II Bathtub
Shower Door: Custom Frameless
Toilet: Kohler Cimmarron
Lights: Norwell Lighting
Drawer Pulls: Top Knobs

Crown Jewel

This Los Angeles homeowner and artist infuses creativity into every aspect of her life. So when determining her powder room's new design, she wanted her guests to feel embraced by enchanting elements inspired by Art Deco and 1940s Hollywood glamour. With lofty dreams but a small workspace, the owner hired Elina Katsioula-Beall of DeWitt Designer Kitchens, Inc., to work her magic.

Katsioula-Beall overcame the room's small dimensions by focusing on the surprising 10-foot ceiling and incorporating a "stepping" technique on the walls, which added dimension through a vertically tiered pattern. The wall adornment continued with the use of rich materials, including cherry wood superimposed with four panels of dramatic mappa-burl. Behind the panels is a Roman travertine tile base, which also follows the same stepping process. The floating, tiered pattern is also seen in the base of the vanity. The stepping-in design motif is duplicated on the ceiling, where hidden rope lighting outlines the motif.

Swarovski crystal handles stemming out of Absolute Black granite punctuates the cupboard vanity. The tall vertical mirror recessed in an alcove creates additional depth. The vanity wall sparkles like a semiprecious stone with tiny glass tile in copper tones, completing the jewel-box feel. *Learn more about this designer at www.dewittdesignerkitchens.com.* «

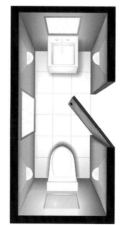

DESIGNER
Elina Katsioula-Beall
DeWitt Designer
Kitchens, Inc.
532 South Lake Ave.
Pasadena, CA 91101
626.792.8833

SPECIAL FEATURES
Jewel box feel and design; rich wall materials, including cherry wood panels superimposed with mappa-burl; cupboard vanity; Swarovski crystal faucets; black granite vanity tops; glass tiling

DIMENSIONS
3'6" x 7'6"

PRODUCTS USED
Flooring: Roman travertine anticato
Vanity: Mappa-burl on black ebony base by Corsi
Vanity Tops: Absolute Black granite by Molise Marble & Granite
Sink: Stainless-steel vessel by Serralina
Faucet: Dornbracht with Swarovski crystal handles
Wallcovering: Mappa-burl and cherry by Corsi, Bizazza tile in copper by Ann Sacks, baseboard in tiered Roman travertine anticato
Toilet: San Raphael by Kohler
Lighting: Low voltage recessed halogens, LED ceiling cove
Hardware: Dornbracht

PHOTOGRAPHER: SUKI MEDENCEVIC

Marble Masterpiece

WHEN IMAGINING A NEW MASTER SUITE, these homeowners sensed that the space's true usefulness could be unlocked by removing outdated features that went underused and unappreciated by their small family of three. When they hired Lee J. Stahl of The Renovated Home, they gained a completely revamped bath with marble and custom accents that evoked lavish simplicity.

The room required a complete gutting to allow for the combination of what was previously a master closet and bar to build the 220-square-foot finished space. With the major construction complete, the bathroom was then swathed in marble and outfitted with the latest products to create a classic feel with a modern twist.

Completing this vision was no easy task due to delicate products such as honey and white onyx and gold Calacatta marble. Stahl and his team spent six weeks on stone fabrication alone to ensure the final result was not only flawless but also made to last.

A complement to the marble touches are top-of-the-line products, including Kallista sinks with Sherle Wagner faucets, a Toto toilet, and P.E. Guerin hardware outfitting the custom cabinetry by The Renovated Home. With the classic and the modern in perfect harmony, the homeowners now have true elegance in their master suite. *Learn more about this designer at www.therenovatedhome.com.* «

DESIGNER
Lee J. Stahl
The Renovated Home
1477 Third Ave.
New York, NY 10028
212.517.7020

SPECIAL FEATURES
Honey and white onyx; gold Calacatta marble; top-of-the-line products

DIMENSIONS
8' x 19'

PRODUCTS USED
Cabinetry: Custom by The Renovated Home
Flooring: Custom border and rug pattern in honey onyx, white onyx, and gold Calacatta marble from Studium
Vanity Tops: 3-centimeter honey onyx
Sinks: Kallista
Faucets: Sherle Wagner
Wallcovering: Custom-cut honey onyx slabs and custom moldings by J and G Marble
Toilet: Toto
Hardware: P.E. Guerin
Mirrors: Medicine cabinetry by the Renovated Home

PHOTOGRAPHER: LEE J. STAHL

Sprawling Suite

THE OWNERS OF THIS PARK AVENUE ABODE had the ample space about which New York City dwellers only dream. The 5,400-square-foot apartment is the result of two combined units. The master bedroom, dressing room, and master bath alone add up to 1,000 square feet. Despite the generous dimensions, the inviting aura the homeowners desired eluded them because the three spaces were separate, rather than contained in one sprawling suite. Lee J. Stahl of The Renovated Home changed that.

The biggest challenge was working within the existing building structure. For the bathroom, he combined the former kitchen, a maid's room, and a maid's bathroom.

The real fun began with the custom touches. The Renovated Home created custom cabinetry, while the rest of the bath was outfitted with custom-cut Calacatta white marble for the wallcovering and floor accents. The finishing touches include a Waterworks tub and Kallista sinks outfitted with Waterworks faucets. The result is a trans-formation that the whole family can enjoy.

Learn more about this designer at www.therenovatedhome.com. «

DESIGNER

Lee J. Stahl
The Renovated Home
1477 Third Ave.
New York, NY 10028
212.517.7020

SPECIAL FEATURES

Revitalized and unique look; custom touches in the cabinetry; Calacatta white marble walls and flooring accents

DIMENSIONS

12' x 15'

PRODUCTS USED

Cabinetry: Custom by The Renovated Home
Flooring: Custom-cut Calacatta white marble with custom border and rug from Studium
Vanity Tops: 3-centimeter Calacatta
Sinks: Kallista
Faucets: Waterworks
Wallcovering: Custom-cut Calacatta white marble
Tub: Waterworks
Toilet: Toto
Mirrors: Custom medicine cabinetry by The Renovated Home

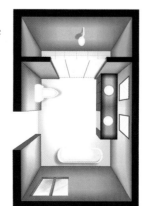

Simply Modern

THIS ALL-NEW MASTER BATHROOM was designed by Mark Lind of CG&S Design-Build as part of a master-suite addition to what was previously a one-story house renovated by CG&S. The master bath revolves around a large central shower with clear glass on all three sides, pebble tile floors, and white glass-tile walls. Directly across from the shower and flanked by tall cabinets, the Jacuzzi tub rests on a plinth of Caesarstone with vertical slot windows on either end—one looking out on a gas fireplace on the roof deck beyond.

A wall-mounted double vanity features a Caesarstone countertop. Custom mirrors are supported on galvanized steel brackets. Adjustable wall-mounted fluorescent fixtures rotate to direct the light at the correct angle. Dark walnut cabinetry and gray tile floors complement the subtle hues of the mosaic wall tile, which adds touches of blue and green in an otherwise neutral palette. Windows are configured as thin vertical slots and high horizontal bands to provide plenty of natural light and privacy at the same time.

Overall, this modern master bath achieves the Zenlike simplicity desired by the owners and provides a sophisticated, serene bathing experience. *Learn more about this designer at www.cgsdb.com.* «

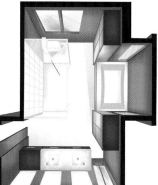

DESIGNER
Mark Lind
CG&S Design-Build
402 Corral Ln.
Austin, TX 78745
512.444.1580

SPECIAL FEATURES
Vertical mosaic glass tile extending from floor to ceiling, filling the entire wall; wall-hung master vanity composed of Caesarstone at the sinks and stained walnut at all other areas; large central shower with clear glass on all three exposed sides

DIMENSIONS
15' x 22'

PRODUCTS USED
Cabinetry: Amazonia Cabinets in walnut
Flooring: DalTile Polished Techno Grey tile
Vanity Tops: Caesarstone in Dusty Stones
Tile: Artistic Tile Serenade Blend glass tile in a mosaic pattern
Sinks: Mirabelle undermount in white porcelain
Faucets: Kohler Margaux in polished chrome
Tub: Jacuzzi Allusion, Pure Air II
Shower Door: Anchor Ventana Glass Company
Toilet: Kohler Strela dual flush in white
Lighting: Birchwood Lighting Kelsey 125, RAB rotating arm bracket, T5 fluorescent lamps
Mirrors: Custom

PHOTOGRAPHER: ANDREW POGUE

Westlake Restoration

OUT OF THE COUNTRY during an extended period of freezing temperatures, these owners returned to their Westlake, Texas, home to find interior water damage caused by burst pipes. To make the most of an unfortunate situation, they redid the house, including the bathroom, to reflect their personal aesthetic and Mission-style decor.

A new dressing room between the master bedroom and bath opens to a walk-in closet and built-in dressers. The master bath, with the original corner closets removed, is now roomy enough for a claw-foot tub, shower, double vanities, and large linen closet.

A high level of design and craftsmanship is seen in the attention to detail throughout the bath. The horizontal bands of stained oak trim around the room line up perfectly with the windows and other woodwork. This was challenging in an older home set into a hillside and with warped floors, out-of-square walls, and out-of-level framing.

The end result of their surprise renovation is an updated, light-filled bath with a Craftsman aesthetic that personifies the owners' design style. *Learn more about this architect at www.cgsdb.com.* «

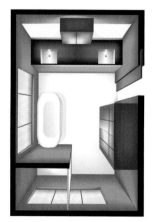

ARCHITECT
Marsha Topham, AIA
Stewart Davis, AIA
CG&S Design-Build
402 Corral Ln.
Austin, TX 78745
512.444.1580

SPECIAL FEATURES
Furniture-grade rift-sawn white oak cabinetry with built-in medicine cabinets, inset doors, and detailed toe kick; warm colors of tile and wood that blend with natural surrounding as seen through prairie-style windows; cove lighting, recessed cans, and Hubbardton Forge sconces that enhance the warm ambience

DIMENSIONS
9' x 14'

PRODUCTS USED
Cabinetry: Custom-made rift-sawn white oak
Flooring: American Olean in Light Smoke
Vanity Tops: Moe Freid Marble and Granite 3-cm honed limestone in Seagrass
Sinks: Kohler Kathryn undercounter lavatory
Tub: Victoria and Albert Como freestanding tub
Toilet: Kohler Kathryn
Lighting: Hubbardton Forge sconces, NSL xenon cove light
Mirrors: Anchor Ventana

Sea-Inspired Suite

WHEN REMODELING THIS 1960S AUSTIN, TEXAS, RANCH HOUSE, these homeowners decided to redo their master suite after one child flew the nest. Having endured many years of a cramped master bathroom, they envisioned a way to get more space without enlarging the footprint of the house. By taking over a former bedroom adjacent to their original bath, the couple imagined expanding and also creating a large dressing room and closet. They hired CG&S Design-Build with whom they collaborated to make their vision a reality. Architect Gregory Thomas, AIA, worked out layout and design details while designer Mark Evans helped select and coordinate finishes.

Corner sinks, cabinets, and mirrors for each spouse flank a central window. There is open shelving for basket storage of bathroom needs. A glass-tile backsplash enlivens the sink area with colorful charm. Glass-block surrounds an enlarged shower; its walls are lined with travertine tile. Pocket doors allow easy movement between the bedroom, bath, and closet, yet offer privacy when it is desired. Tile most often used as swimming pool liner graces the floor of the bathroom, acting as a colorful, complementary neighbor to the Saltillo tile of the closet and bedrooms. The room's watery, cool palette creates a soothing retreat reminiscent of the sea. *Learn more about this designer at www.cgsdb.com.* «

ARCHITECT/DESIGNER
Gregory Thomas, AIA
Mark Evans
CG&S Design-Build
402 Corral Ln.
Austin, TX 78745
512.444.1580

SPECIAL FEATURES
Unique use of color; custom hickory cabinets and trim; medicine cabinets; open shelves with baskets; corner sinks and mirrors; glass-block shower enclosure; glass backsplash tile in water colors; pool tile as floor tile

DIMENSIONS
7'6" x 9'11"

PRODUCTS USED
Cabinetry: Custom hickory cabinets by Amazonia Cabinetry
Flooring: Mosaic tile by Cepac Tile in Blue Satin
Backsplash Tile: Lunada Bay Japonaise Series glass tile in Pear Garden Natural
Shower Wall Tile: Ivory vein-cut travertine
Glass Block: Pittsburg Corning Decora
Vanity Tops: Sunfire 3-centimeter granite with polished finish
Sinks: China Shell undermount trough sink
Plumbing Fixtures: Hansgrohe Montreux wall-mount sink faucet
Toilet: Kohler Persuade dual-flush comfort-height toilet
Lighting: Halo recessed lighting, Pottery Barn sconce
Hardware: B & M Hardware in brushed nickel
Mirrors: Anchor Ventana
Window: Pella Architect Series with obscure glass

Bryker Bungalow

THE NEW OWNERS of this Bryker Woods bungalow in Austin, Texas, wanted to create an en suite bath that complemented the Asian accents in their home. Originally using the single bath located off the hall and small closets in separate bedrooms, they also wanted new storage that would accommodate both of their wardrobes.

The 244-square-foot addition at the rear of the home includes a new master bath now reached from the bedroom. The new space's small footprint called for an efficient configuration that would include a walk-in shower, a toilet area, a vanity with double sinks, and a dressing area with built-in alder cabinetry. A linen cabinet dividing the vanity area from the toilet area provides additional storage. Because the new bath backs up to the glass-block window of the existing one, a skylight was placed above the shower, bringing light to both spaces.

The new light-filled master bath with cool walls, clean lines, and granite and tile finishes is a welcome addition for the owners and is well suited to the style of their home. *Learn more about this architect at www.cgsdb.com.* «

ARCHITECT
Marsha Topham, AIA
CG&S Design-Build
402 Corral Ln.
Austin, TX 78745
512.444.1580

SPECIAL FEATURES
Skylight above shower illuminating both new and existing bath; stained alder cabinets for ample storage of clothing and linens; good lighting and an open plan to make small rooms feel spacious; shower niche with accent tiles for a focal point

DIMENSIONS
12' x 13'

PRODUCTS USED
Cabinetry: Custom-built stained Alder
Flooring: Daltile Cremona Caffe mosaic
Vanity Tops: Moe Freid Marble and Granite 2-centimeter Costa Esmeralda granite
Sinks: Proflo
Shower Door: Anchor Ventana
Toilet: Kohler Cimerron
Lighting: Juno recessed cans
Mirrors: Framed mirrors

PHOTOGRAPHER: TRE DUNHAM

Bathroom with a View

DESIGNER
Mark Lind
CG&S Design-Build
402 Corral Ln.
Austin, TX 78745
512.444.1580

SPECIAL FEATURES
A continuous bank of windows to maximize views; custom, freestanding mirrors that are designed to match the design and finish of the decorative light fixtures; an all-glass shower/tub zone to allow views of the hills beyond

DIMENSIONS
13' x 12'

PRODUCTS USED
Cabinetry: Amazonia Cabinets in alder
Flooring: Slate in a herringbone pattern for room, black slate in a herringbone pattern for shower
Vanity Tops and Tub Deck: Bardiglio marble
Sinks: Mirabelle undermount in white china
Plumbing Fixtures: Hansgrohe Solaris E
Tub: Kohler Tea for Two
Glass: Anchor Ventana
Toilet: Kohler Cimarron
Lighting: Halo recessed, Hubbarton Forge suspended, Kakomi pendants, opal glass
Mirrors: Custom

SADDLED WITH DATED TILE, WALLPAPER, AND CABINETRY; a little-used corner tub that took up valuable space; and small, leaking windows, this second-story master bath needed a redo. The owners, both geology professors, asked Mark Lind of CG&S Design-Build to increase the size of the shower, expand the river views, and use natural finishes.

Now, a combined shower and tub provide a more generous bathing area, and the frameless glass enclosure contains water without obstructing views afforded by the large horizontal bank of windows, which expose the river but maintain privacy. The soffit unifies the space and provides for both cove and down lighting. The vanity mirrors are suspended in front of the windows on custom-made brackets that match the light fixtures.

Natural-stone materials were used throughout, including marble walls and tub surround, slate floors, and granite countertops. Attention to detail and craftsmanship can be seen in the horizontal band of glass accent tiles that defines the room's perimeter. The owners are pleased with the generously sized bathing area and views that now wrap the corner of the house. The space is better utilized, and the stone finishes reflect the professional interests of the owners. The finished master bath is infused with light and nature—both inside and out! *Learn more about this designer at www.cgsdb.com.* «

Staying Faithful

THIS 1930S TWO-BEDROOM, two-bathroom bungalow in Austin, Texas, underwent its last face-lift in the 1950s. So the homeowners brought Royce Flournoy of Texas Construction Company on board to expand, renovate, and revamp their historic home, so long overdue for an update.

The client's goal: to create a new master suite filled with dramatic upgrades—all while remaining true to the original 1930s architecture. An avid antique collector, the owner was eager to incorporate many of her favorite pieces acquired through the years. This design decision brought a personal touch to the space while maintaining the character of the older home.

In the new master suite's bathroom, antique marble washbasins were restored and repurposed as stunning, one-of-a-kind sinks. One of the owner's prized antique mirrors was rotated and used over the vanity. Providing light by the mirror doubles the illumination in the room and provides brilliant reflections from two antique light fixtures that were rewired as pendents.

In the end, this 80-year-old abode received a renewed look while staying faithful to its historic roots.

Learn more about this general contractor at www.txconstruct.com. «

GENERAL CONTRACTOR
Royce Flournoy
Texas Construction
Company
4622 Burnet Rd.
Austin, TX 78756
512.451.8050

SPECIAL FEATURES
Antique marble washbasins restored for use as bathroom sinks; a prized antique mirror of the client's was rotated and used as the vanity mirror; two antique light fixtures rewired as pendent lights at the vanity

DIMENSIONS
9' x 17'

PRODUCTS USED
Cabinetry: Paint-grade, raised-panel, face-framed cabinetry
Flooring: Marble
Vanity Tops: Marble
Sinks: Restored antique washbasins
Plumbing Fixtures: Kohler
Tub: Kohler Tea for Two
Shower Door: Frameless ½-inch clear glass
Toilet: Kohler Memoirs
Lighting: Antique pendent lights
Mirrors: Antique mirror selected by client

PHOTOGRAPHER: COLES HAIRSTON

A Modern Makeover

GENERAL CONTRACTOR
Royce Flournoy
Texas Construction
Company
4622 Burnet Rd.
Austin, TX 78756
512.451.8050

SPECIAL FEATURES
Clerestory window above shower and tub area for ample natural light; Bisazza White glass mosaic blend tile for tub and shower surround; crisp, clean transitions between vanity light, mirror, and counter

DIMENSIONS
10' x 12'

PRODUCTS USED
Cabinetry: Paint-grade maple
Flooring: Red Oak sanded and finished on-site
Vanity Tops: Carrera marble
Sinks: Kohler Ladena
Plumbing Fixtures: Dornbracht
Tub: Kohler Tea for Two
Shower Door: Clear frameless shower glass
Toilet: Duravit Stark
Lighting: Artemide basic bath strip
Hardware: Hafele
Mirrors: Custom-cut glass mirror

READY TO REVAMP their Tudor-style home, these Austin, Texas, homeowners had two major desires for the redesign: one, they wanted to increase the square footage of their floor plan, and two, they wanted to incorporate contemporary design elements amid the traditional architecture. To walk this fine style line while expanding the space, they hired local expert Royce Flournoy of Texas Construction Company.

As Flournoy undertook renovating the existing home, he planned the addition of a utility, study, and master suite. For the master bathroom, he incorporated the use of mosaic tile, marble counters, and European-style cabinetry—all materials that were contemporary yet complementary to the home's original style. Specifically, Bisazza White glass mosaic tile adds interest to the tub and shower surround. Crisp, clean transitions between the vanity light, mirror, and counter update the vanity detail. And a clerestory window above the shower and tub area allows ample natural light to enter.

Beautifully blending the new with the old, Flournoy pulled off this remodeling and restyling project seamlessly. And the homeowners got exactly what they wanted and more: a house addition that made room for modern living.

Learn more about this general contractor at www.txconstruct.com. «

PHOTOGRAPHER: COLES HAIRSTON

Revived Austin Bungalow

When these Austin, Texas, residents began renovations on their second home, they knew they had their work cut out for them. Their 1924 bungalow-style home fit in charmingly with the eclectic Austin backdrop, but it needed modernizing to fit the homeowners' lifestyle and sensibilities. The perfect place to start was with a second-story addition to a master suite. The owners hired David Wilkes of David Wilkes Builders to spearhead the task of remodeling their Jazz Age dwelling.

In the bathroom, Wilkes installed custom oil-rubbed walnut cabinets and a custom oil-rubbed barn door, which contrasts nicely with the otherwise bright white tile of the bath and makes the transition to the master bedroom, with its rift-sawn (straight grain) antique-white oak flooring and staircase, seamless. Other updates include the Kohler vessel sink with stainless-steel faucet and a walnut vanity with a Raven Caesarstone countertop. Kohler is also represented in the deep sunken tub, while the Anchor Ventana shower is outfitted with a custom-cut glass door and shower bench.

One of the greatest hurdles in modernizing an older home lies in tackling the bathroom, but Wilkes and his team passed this test with excellence. *Learn more about this general contractor at www.davidwilkesbuilders.com.* «

GENERAL CONTRACTOR
David Wilkes
David Wilkes Builders
5450 Bee Caves Rd.
Ste. 4B
Austin, TX 78746
512.328.9888

SPECIAL FEATURES
Custom oil-rubbed walnut cabinets; custom oil-rubbed barn door; rift-sawn antique-white oak flooring and staircase

DIMENSIONS
15' x 15'

PRODUCTS USED
Cabinetry: Custom-built oil-rubbed walnut
Vanity Tops: 3-centimeter Caesarstone in Raven
Sinks: Kohler
Plumbing Fixtures: Kohler
Tub: Kohler
Shower Door: Custom-cut glass door, Anchor Ventana
Toilet: Toto White Aquia elongated bowl, Toto White Aquia tank, Toto Cotton elongated soft seat

PHOTOGRAPHER: THOMAS MCCONNELL

From Past to Present

WALKING DOWN THE STREETS of the Hyde Park neighborhood in Austin, Texas, is like strolling through another era. Originally built in 1891, the historic area is considered the city's first suburb and is still a favorite today, thanks to the residents' preservation efforts. But while charm makes up for a lot of the challenges associated with owning an older home, it doesn't cover everything, such as having only one bathroom—and an outdated one at that.

This was the situation that spurred this remodeling project. Contacting local builder David Wilkes of David Wilkes Builders, this homeowner was ready to complete the long-overdue update to give the master bathroom modern-day amenities and a refreshed aesthetic.

While there are often special considerations when working on older homes, Wilkes's biggest challenge presented itself in the form of a tight turnaround time—necessary because there is only one bathroom in the home. He was able to complete the reconfiguration without sparing any style. A purposeful lack of a shower enclosure visually enlarges the room. Specially chosen materials fill the space with stunning surfaces, which are accented with complementary fixtures and flourishes—all details that bring this bathroom from past to present.

Learn more about this general contractor at www.davidwilkesbuilders.com. «

GENERAL CONTRACTOR
David Wilkes
David Wilkes Builders
5450 Bee Caves Rd.
Ste. 4B
Austin, TX 78746
512.328.9888

SPECIAL FEATURES
Lack of shower enclosure for the appearance of a larger bathroom

DIMENSIONS
6' x 12'

PRODUCTS USED
Cabinetry: Oak plywood with dark gray stain and alpha finish on full overlay cabinet, vertical stiles with inset frame
Flooring: Apple stone honed
Vanity Tops: CaesarStone polished concrete
Sink: Whitehaus overmount oval basin
Plumbing Fixtures: Kohler Stillness faucet and tub faucet, Kohler showerhead, Kohler Flipside handshower
Tub: Kaldewei Sani-form
Toilet: Existing Toto toilet
Lighting: Restoration Hardware Spritz single sconces, ceiling-mounted recessed cans
Hardware: Restoration Hardware Chatam double robe hook in polished nickel; Restoration Hardware Asbury single towel bar, tissue roll holder in polished nickel, and linen cabinet pulls in polished nickel
Mirrors: Restoration Hardware Asbury standard oval mirror in polished nickel

PHOTOGRAPHER: THOMAS MCCONNELL

Period Update

LOCATED IN THE HEART OF AUSTIN, TEXAS, just north of the University of Texas, Hyde Park originated in 1891 and, as mentioned on page 222, is considered to be the city's first suburb. Just as many of the homes in this historic district are marked by the charms of years past, they are also saddled with some of the shortcomings of older styles. This was the case in this Hyde Park home, where the master bathroom was cramped and dated.

To upgrade and upsize the space to meet modern standards, this homeowner hired David Wilkes of David Wilkes Builders for the job. His task: the remodel and expansion of the existing master bathroom as well as the addition of a small porch—all while upholding the historical style. The new scope provided a much better layout for a more function-friendly bathroom. Plus, the new porch provides access to the garden, which is a favorite feature for the client, who is an avid gardener.

To preserve the home's history in the design, the client selected period fixtures. Wilkes converted an antique dresser into a functional vanity with a lav, installed long-leaf hardwood floors to match the bedroom, and re-created existing trim conditions for continuity of details. All of these efforts resulted in the successful remodel of this historic house. *Learn more about this general contractor at www. davidwilkesbuilders.com.* «

GENERAL CONTRACTOR
David Wilkes
David Wilkes Builders
5450 Bee Caves Rd.
Ste. 4B
Austin, TX 78746
512.328.9888

SPECIAL FEATURES
Period fixtures to continue the appearance of the existing home; a reworked antique dresser converted into a functional vanity; long-leaf hardwood floors to match the bedroom; re-created existing trim conditions for continuity of details

DIMENSIONS
6' x 12'

PRODUCTS USED
Flooring: Long-leaf pine wood
Vanity: Custom-made from antique dresser
Plumbing Fixtures: Period-style fixtures
Tub: Existing claw foot freestanding tub
Mirrors: Antique hanging mirror by owner

PHOTOGRAPHER: THOMAS MCCONNELL

Hotel Service at Home

ALTHOUGH THEIR WESTLAKE Hills, Texas, home's master bathroom contains the basics, the homeowners wanted to upgrade its amenities. Ready to remodel, they hired David Wilkes of David Wilkes Builders to add style and increase the room's functionality.

Specifically, the clients wanted a spa-style bath with a service level on par with a five-star hotel suite, where everything they need is easily accessible. Because their master suite is located on the second floor, they wanted to eliminate all the trips up and down the stairs while getting ready in the mornings and unwinding in the evenings. This meant that the coffee and other accoutrements needed to come upstairs.

While its second-story locale posed some access challenges during construction, the designer's solutions kept the project on track. He incorporated a coffee station as well as an undercounter refrigerator into the design, so the clients could have a cup brewing while bathing. Adding to the hotel ambiance, the vanity cabinets were kept off the floor and undercabinet lighting was added. With the bathroom rebuilt, these homeowners are enjoying hotel-style service right at home. *Learn more about this general contractor at www.davidwilkesbuilders.com.* «

GENERAL CONTRACTOR
David Wilkes
David Wilkes Builders
5450 Bee Caves Rd.
Ste. 4B
Austin, TX 78746
512.328.9888

SPECIAL FEATURES
Coffee station and undercounter refrigerator, designed for a hotel experience; vanity cabinets raised off the floor; undercabinet lighting for a warmer feel

DIMENSIONS
10' x 22'

PRODUCTS USED
Cabinetry: Custom-made stained mahogany cabinets
Flooring: Durango, Architectural Tile & Stone
Vanity Tops: Silestone Blanco Maple with T20 Eased Edge
Sinks: Kohler Caxton Oval sink in White Kohler Purist widespread lav faucet with cross handles in polished chrome for tub and hand-held on-deck Stillness Handshower; Rain Head with hand-held on hook and cross handles for shower; Handshower, Supply elbow; Stillness hook, hose; rain head with contemporary arm
Shower Door: Custom-made frameless glass shower enclosure
Toilet: Toto Pacifica
Lighting: Sconces, cirrus by designer; sconces at vanity, robbia or equal by designer
Hardware: All by designer
Mirrors: Custom-cut mirrors

PHOTOGRAPHER: THOMAS MCCONNELL

Hill Country Masterpiece

FOR MANY, THE THOUGHT OF DESIGNING and building a home is a life-long dream. For these homeowners, it became a dream come true when they chose a lot located on the 12th fairway of the Austin Country Club in Texas. Although it was a difficult site on a steep hill, it created unique design opportunities for James LaRue of James D. LaRue Architects.

Complete with a pool, outdoor dining area, and seating groupings that naturally blend into the surrounding environment, the homeowners have all the luxuries of a new home with the stunning backdrop of the hillside landscape. The careful positioning of the house paired with an abundance of floor to ceiling windows achieves the goal of constructing a sophisticated yet livable house.

Blending in perfectly with the contemporary and warm appearance of the rest of the home is the impressive master bath. Outfitted throughout with top-of-the-line materials—from the flat-panel hanging walnut cabinets by Cabinet Design and Manufacturing to the bright and inviting Fabrique tile flooring in Crème Linen by DalTile and the vanity tops by Renaissance Stone Work in Bama White—the bath is a place where the homeowners can rejuvenate in a relaxing setting. Topped off with an MTI Whirlpool Tub, the bath truly completes the vision of the home. *Learn more about this architect at www.larue-architects.com.* «

ARCHITECT
James D. LaRue
James D. LaRue
Architects
500 N. Capital of TX
Hwy., Bldg. 8, Ste. 110
Austin, TX 78746
512.347.1688

SPECIAL FEATURES
Hill Country
contemporary design
that opens up to a golf
course view

DIMENSIONS
13' x 19'

PRODUCTS USED
Cabinetry: Cabinet
Design and
Manufacturing, flat-
panel hanging walnut
cabinets
Flooring: DalTile
Fabrique Crème Linen
Vanity Tops:
Renaissance Stone Work
in Bama White
Sinks: Kohler
Plumbing Fixtures:
Kohler, Hansgrohe
Tub: MTI Whirlpool
Shower Door: Custom
Glass
Toilet: Kohler
Lighting: Lighting Inc.
Hardware: Ginger and
Top Knobs Hopewell
Collection
Mirrors: Anchor Ventana

PHOTOGRAPHER: COLES HAIRSTON

Rustic Ranch

WHEN THESE EMPTY NESTERS planned a move back to their home state of Texas, they did so in style, building a home in the equestrian community of Horseshoe Bay. Hired to design the house were Rick Burleson and David Costea of Burleson Design Group–Architects.

The site contained mature oaks, so the house was designed to fit among the existing trees. The result is a house in sync with both nature and the homeowners' rustic ranch style. Though there are many unique aspects of the home, the master bath truly captures the homeowners' goal for their dwelling, matching their simple style with modern luxury.

His and her vanities are a treat afforded by the room's spaciousness. The custom cabinetry was constructed locally, and the vanities are each topped with native quarried granite and outfitted with Kohler sinks and indirect lighting alcoves. The granite tops complement the honed- and stained-concrete floors with leaf imprints, creating a warm and contemporary atmosphere. The luxury is continued in the bath's walk-in shower, which features stone-faced pedestals that serve as shelf space for shower sundries. With an abundance of stylish features, it is clear that this design excels in both contemporary function and rustic ranch form. *Learn more about this architect at www.burlesondesigngroup.com.* «

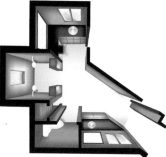

ARCHITECT
Rick Burleson
Burleson Design Group–
Architects
111 Old Kyle Rd.
Ste. 208
Wimberley, TX 78676
512.842.1308

SPECIAL FEATURES
His and her vanity areas with indirect lighting alcoves; walk-in shower with stone-faced pedestals; honed concrete floor with oak leaf imprints; closets with internal dressing areas

DIMENSIONS
18' x 20'

PRODUCTS USED
Cabinetry: Locally constructed custom cabinets
Flooring: Honed and stained concrete
Vanity Tops: Locally quarried granite
Sinks: Kohler

PHOTOGRAPHER: DANIEL NADLEBACH

At-Home Retreat

WITH A BUSY LIFESTYLE often calling them away from home, this couple wanted to make the time they spend there as restful and restorative as possible. In line with this vision was a complete bathroom remodel completed by Leslie Fine of Leslie Fine Interiors, Inc., who transformed the space into a spalike retreat.

Fine began the project by completely shaking up the preexisting layout of the master bath, which was originally a confined space of four separate areas. What was left in the wake of these changes was a completely open floor plan. By removing the walls between the separate rooms, the space was made more functional and inviting. Now rather than feeling closed-in, the space is flooded with natural light. Additional light is provided by the pendant fixtures, which also mimic the effect of the newly-installed two-sided stainless-steel mirror that hangs from the ceiling. This mirror design helps support the unusual back-to-back vanity configuration, which is in the center of the room, without crowding the space.

Adding to the beauty of the spalike design is the mosaic and limestone tile within the shower and behind the makeup table. To show off this touch, the shower was outfitted with custom glass doors. *Learn more about this designer at www.lesliefineinteriors.com.* «

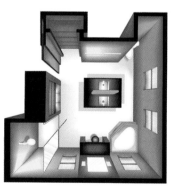

DESIGNER
Leslie Fine
Leslie Fine Interiors, Inc.
224 Clarendon St.,
Ste. 61
Boston, MA 02116
617.236.2286

SPECIAL FEATURES
Spalike retreat created through an open floor plan; mosaic tile, vanity, and two-sided stainless-steel mirrors

DIMENSIONS
18'7" x 18'4"

PRODUCTS USED
Large Tile: Ann Sacks Linen
Mosaic Tile: Ann Sacks Zen Weave
Center Vanity: Poggenpohl
Makeup Vanity: Poggenpohl
Pendants: Tech Lighting Essex
Hanging Mirror: Custom

PHOTOGRAPHER: MICHAEL J. LEE

Urban Appeal

WHEN CHOOSING THE PERFECT BACHELOR PAD, this owner wanted to avoid the pitfalls of suburbia and instead went for a newly built, modern apartment in the recently gentrified part of town. Designed with sleek and simple sophistication in mind, the apartment reflects the owner's own professional style and minimalist tastes.

The modern design of the apartment extends to the master bath, where rich graphite hues in the cabinetry and vanity top play off the neutral creams and whites. The large floor tiles match the walls in the tub and shower space. The floor-length window and recessed light fixtures illuminate the space while providing a calm and peaceful atmosphere.

The narrowness of the room is downplayed by the use of light and color, along with the strategic placement of the other amenities, from the wall-length vanity and toilet on one side to the deep white ceramic tub and custom glass-enclosed shower on the other. Atop the vanity are two Kohler oval vessel sinks with stainless-steel faucets. There's a recessed full-length mirror on the wall. A heated towel rack is another highlight that adds to the comforting space.

With the pairing of the simple lines, neutral colors, and top-of-the-line products, the bathroom has become one of the owner's favorite rooms. «

SPECIAL FEATURES
Sophisticated, contemporary design achieved through the latest products and neutral hues

DIMENSIONS
8' x 14'

PRODUCTS USED
Cabinetry: Wall-length locally built custom cabinets
Flooring: Large tiles
Vanity Tops: Graphite hued tops
Sinks: Kohler vessel sinks
Plumbing Fixtures: Kohler
Tub: Kohler
Shower Door: Custom built glass
Toilet: Kohler
Lighting: Recessed and natural

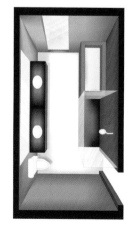

Tribeca Refurbishment

THIS NEW YORK CITY COUPLE wanted the ideal home for raising their young family and found it in a renovated Tribeca loft dating back to 1892. The age and structure of the building, which was originally a masonry warehouse, had beautiful yet challenging existing conditions for the firm KATZ Architecture and interior designer Warren Red. Part of the overall project included the addition of two new bathrooms.

For the master bath, the existing structure and 3-foot-thick walls made it difficult to install plumbing, so all of the fixtures had to be located on one wall. To overcome the narrow room created by this linear arrangement, the team installed a curved door at the end of the bathroom. It also helped to soften the exterior appearance of floor-to-ceiling walnut paneling. Wall fixtures create a greater sense of uninterrupted openness.

The floor and back wall were surfaced with a visually striated marble that draws the eye across the wall. The back wall is now a focal point. *Learn more about this designer at www.warrenred.com. Learn more about this architect at www.katzarch.com.* «

DESIGNER
Warren Red, Interior Designer
611 Broadway, Ste. 319
New York, NY 10012
917.620.9525

KATZ Architecture
611 Broadway, Ste. 834
New York, NY 10012
212.353.1080

SPECIAL FEATURES
Marble finishes; curved door; the room's proportions

DIMENSIONS
5'6" x 9'6"

PRODUCTS USED
Cabinetry: Custom lacquer base cabinet by GC, Robern Medicine cabinet
Flooring: Linak striated marble slab from Stone Source
Sink: Rapsel Kanal Sink
Faucets: Dornbracht Lulu
Wallcovering: Linak striated marble slab from Stone Source; Bianco Dolomiti wall tile from Stone Source
Tub: Kohler Tea for Two
Tub Filler: Quarto by Artos (F202-1 In Wall Tub Spout)
Shower Set: Dornbracht Lulu
Toilet: Duravit Starck 2
Bidet: Duravit Starck 2

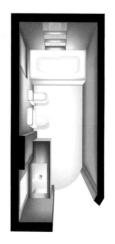

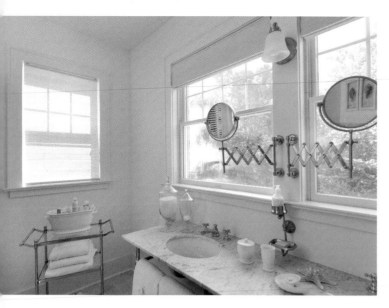

An Inviting Retreat

WHEN CREATING THE PERFECT GUEST BATH, these homeowners envisioned something inviting and luxurious that would match the simple elegance in the rest of the home. To achieve this, they enlisted Guillaume Gentet of Décor by Guillaume Gentet.

The new bath was not without challenges. The room's almost wall-to-wall windows flooded the space with natural light but also created a logistical hurdle in terms of placing the vanity and mirrors. To overcome this, Gentet and his team built a custom vanity and installed extension mirrors from Restoration Hardware in place of traditional wall-mounted ones. Outfitted in white Carrara marble with base chrome pipes, the result is a clean look that adds a twist to a classic design. The room is enhanced by Artistic Tile floors in muted greens and tans and the subtle wall color, "Daiquiri Ice" by Benjamin Moore.

A focal point of the guest bath is the vintage armoire. Picked up by Gentet at a New York City flea market, it is a clever solution to storing bath essentials without creating a cluttered look—especially important in this simple design. *Learn more about this designer at www.guillaumegentet.com.* «

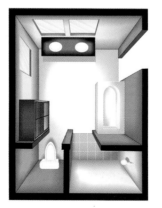

DESIGNER
Guillaume Gentet
Décor by Guillaume
Gentet
139 Fulton St., Ste. 417
New York, NY 10038
212.571.1040

SPECIAL FEATURES
Large windows; vintage
touches; custom sinks
and vanity; radiant
heating

DIMENSIONS
10' x 12'

PRODUCTS USED
Cabinetry: Vintage
armoire
Flooring: Artistic Tile
Vanity Tops: Custom with
white Carrara marble,
base chrome pipes
Sinks: Kohler
Plumbing Fixtures:
Restoration Hardware
faucets
Tub: Kohler
Shower: Tiles from South
Hampton Brick and Tile,
Showerhead: efaucets
Toilet: Kohler
Mirrors: Restoration
Hardware
Wallcovering: Benjamin
Moore oil-based paint in
Daiquiri Ice

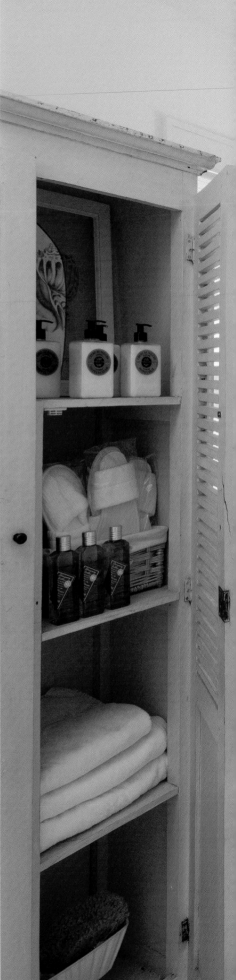

PHOTOGRAPHER: ALEX KROKE

If you like **Best Signature Baths,** look for these
and other fine **Creative Homeowner books** wherever books are sold.

**Decorating: The Smart Approach
to Design**
All you need to know to design your
home like a pro. Over 350 photos.
288 pp.; 8½" x 10⅞"
BOOK #: CH279680

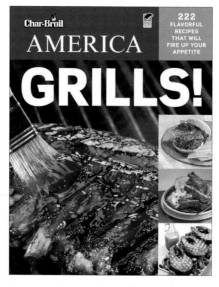

Char-Broil's America Grills!
Flavorful grilling recipes, including
appetizers, entrees, side dishes, and
desserts. Over 335 photos.
304 pp.; 8½" x 10⅞"
BOOK #: CH253050

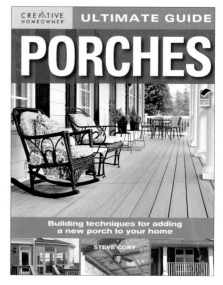

Ultimate Guide: Porches
Step-by-step guide to design and build
a porch. Over 300 photos and illos.
192 pp.; 8½" x 10⅞"
BOOK #: CH277970

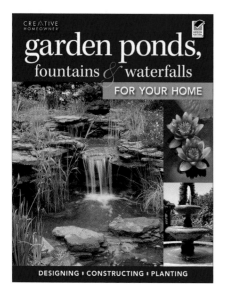

**Garden Ponds, Fountains & Waterfalls for
Your Home**
Secrets to creating garden features. Over
490 photos and illos. 256 pp.; 8½" x 10⅞"
BOOK #: CH274450

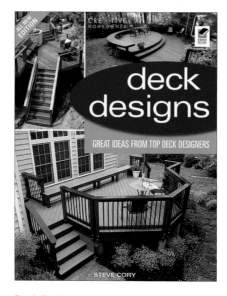

Deck Designs
Plans from top deck designers & builders.
Over 480 photos and illustrations.
240 pp.; 8½" x 10⅞"
BOOK #: CH277382

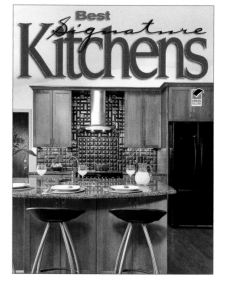

Best Signature Kitchens
Inspiring kitchens from top designers.
Over 250 photos.
240 pp; 8¼" x 10⅞"
BOOK #: CH279510

For more information and to order direct, go to **www.creativehomeowner.com**